A to Z: Everything You Need to Know about LinkedIn® for Business Owners & Leaders

Published by Crossbridge Books
Worcester
www.crossbridgeeducational.com
© Crossbridge Books 2024

ISBN: 978 1 916945 05 0

British Library Cataloguing in Publication Data. A catalogue record for this book is available from the British Library.

LinkedIn is the registered trademark of LinkedIn Corporation or its affiliates. The use of the LinkedIn trademark in connection with this product does not signify any affiliation with or endorsement by LinkedIn Corporation or its affiliates.

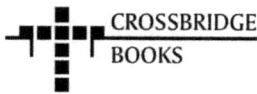

CROSSBRIDGE
BOOKS

The information provided in this book is accurate and up-to-date as of the time of publication. However, please be aware that online platforms, including LinkedIn®, are constantly evolving, and features, functionalities, and best practices may change over time. While every effort has been made to ensure the content is relevant and helpful, the author or publisher cannot be held responsible for any discrepancies or changes that may occur after the publication date. Readers are encouraged to verify information and stay informed about updates on the platforms discussed. This book is not endorsed by Linkedin®.

Cover photo by KoolShooters

A to Z: Everything You Need to Know about LinkedIn® for Business Owners & Leaders

Esther Partridge -Warner
BSc(Hons) PgCE LTHE FHEA

Table of Contents

Table of Contents

Table of Contents

Table of Contents

Table of Contents

Introduction

Welcome to 'A to Z: Everything You Need to Know about LinkedIn® for Business Owners and Leaders'.

In this book, we will explore the powerful potential of LinkedIn® as a dynamic platform for business owners and leaders looking to elevate their professional presence, engage with their audience, and drive growth. Whether you are a seasoned entrepreneur, a small business owner, a start-up founder, or a business leader, this guide is designed specifically for you. If you're ready to transform your LinkedIn™ profile from a digital CV into a vibrant hub of opportunity, you're in the right place.

In today's ever-evolving digital landscape, LinkedIn® is more than just a networking site; it's a bustling marketplace of ideas, connections, and possibilities. However, navigating this platform can feel overwhelming, much like preparing for a big party. This book aims to demystify LinkedIn® providing you with actionable strategies and insights to help you stand out, build meaningful relationships, and ultimately, celebrate your successes.

You might wonder why I've chosen a party analogy to guide our exploration of LinkedIn™. The answer is simple: just as a successful party brings people together, creates memorable experiences, and fosters connections, your presence on LinkedIn® should do the same. Think of your LinkedIn® profile as the ultimate party invitation, a chance to showcase your unique personality, skills, and offerings to the world.

Every topic in this book will draw parallels between the elements of a great party and effective strategies for leveraging LinkedIn®. We'll explore how to set the right atmosphere with your profile, curate engaging content that keeps your audience dancing, and use networking techniques that create lasting connections. Just as a DJ reads the crowd and adapts the music to keep the energy high, you'll learn how to engage with your audience in a way that resonates and inspires.

By embracing this party analogy, I hope to make the process of mastering LinkedIn® not only informative but also enjoyable.

So, let's turn up the music, light up the dance floor, and get ready to take your LinkedIn® presence to the next level. Together, we'll create a vibrant and engaging experience that transforms your connections into lasting relationships and your business into a thriving success!

Best wishes
Esther

August 2024

How to use this book

This book is designed to provide a unique, personalised learning experience that adapts to your specific needs and interests.

Here's how to get the best from this innovative format:

Understanding the Structure

Non-Linear Reading: Unlike traditional books, you won't read this from cover to cover. Instead, you'll navigate through the content based on your choices.

Choice Points: At the end of each section, you'll be presented with two or more options. For example:
  - If you want to learn more about 'Profile Optimisation', turn to page 117.
  - If you're interested in 'Content Strategy', turn to page 34.

Personalised Journey: Your choices will create a unique path through the book, tailoring the content to your specific interests and needs.

Getting the Most from Your Experience

1. Start with Your Goals: Begin by identifying what you want to achieve on LinkedIn®. This will help guide your choices throughout the book. Maybe start on page 212.

2. Explore Multiple Paths: Don't hesitate to go back and make different choices to explore various aspects of LinkedIn® strategy.

3. Take Notes: As you navigate through the book, jot down key insights and action items relevant to your business.

4. Implement as You Go: Try applying the strategies you learn immediately to your LinkedIn® activities for real-time learning and improvement.

5. Use Bookmarks: Mark important pages or sections you want to revisit later.

Remember, there's no 'right' or 'wrong' way to use this book. Your journey across the dance floor of LinkedIn® will be as unique as your business needs. So, feel free to explore different moves and grooves.

Enjoy the rhythm of discovering new strategies and may your adventure lead to a spectacular business success that lights up the disco ball.

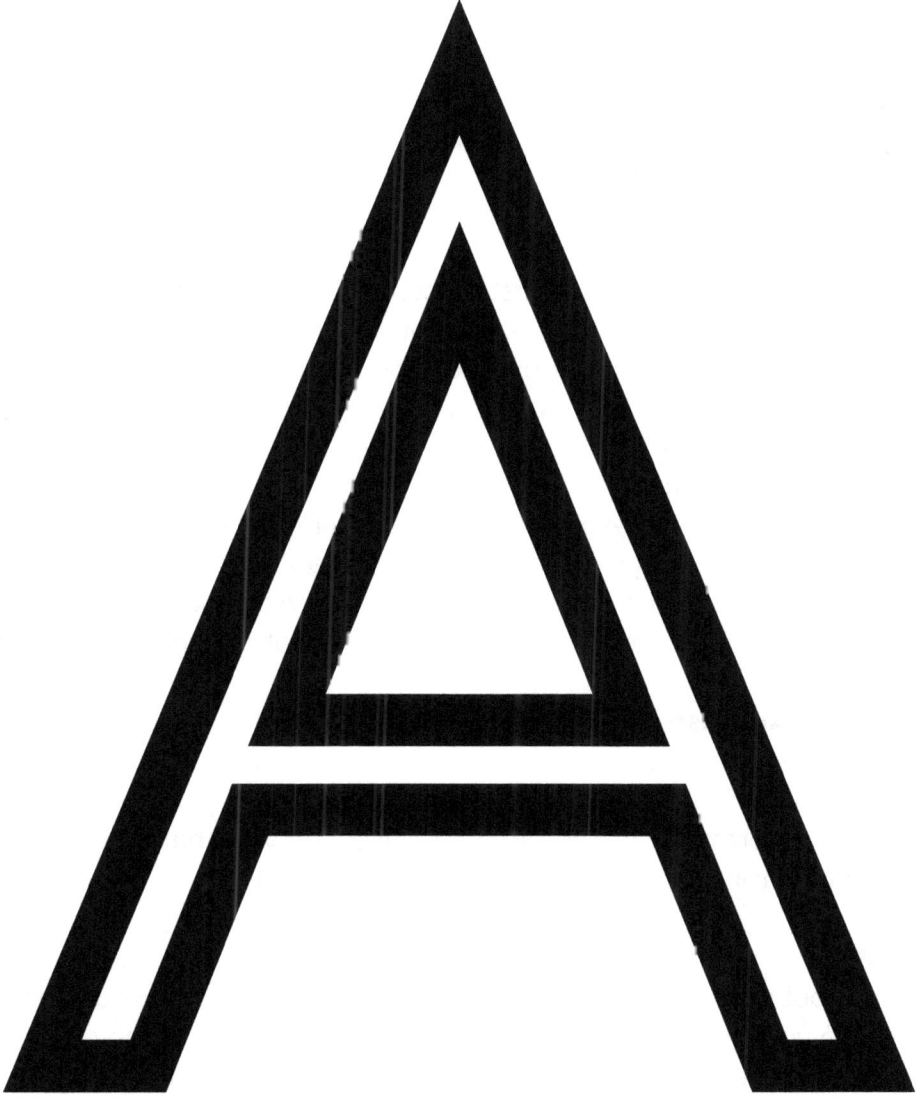

1. ABOUT SECTION

A

The About section on LinkedIn™ is your opportunity to shine like a disco ball, reflecting your unique personality, skills, and the essence of your business. This section serves as a personal introduction, allowing you to tell your story and showcase what sets you apart in your industry. Just as a DJ captures the crowd's attention with their distinctive sound and style, your About section is crucial for making a memorable first impression for potential clients and connections.

Importance of the About Section

First Impressions Matter
The About section is often one of the first places people look when visiting your profile. It's your chance to make a strong impression, much like the opening track at a party that sets the tone for the night. A well-crafted About section can draw people in and encourage them to explore your profile further.

Showcasing Your Personality
This section also allows you to express your personality and passion for your work. Just as a DJ's unique flair can energise a dance floor, your authentic voice can resonate with your audience, making them more likely to connect with you. Sharing your journey, values, and vision helps potential clients and partners relate to you on a personal level.

Highlighting Your Expertise
The About section is an excellent place to outline your skills, experiences, and areas of expertise. By clearly articulating what you bring to the table, you position yourself as a credible source of information in your field, similar to the way that a DJ establishes their reputation by showcasing their musical knowledge and skill.

Building Trust
A compelling About section builds trust with your audience. When you share your story and demonstrate your expertise, it reassures potential clients that they are dealing with a knowledgeable professional. This trust is similar to the confidence party-goers feel when they know they're in the hands of a skilled DJ who knows how to keep the party alive.

Encouraging Engagement
A well-written About section can prompt readers to reach out, ask questions, or start conversations. Just as a DJ engages the crowd with calls to action, such as inviting them to dance or join in on the fun, your About section can encourage visitors to connect with you, leading to valuable networking opportunities.

ABOUT SECTION

A

How to Craft an Effective About Section

1. Start with a Hook: Begin with an engaging opening that captures attention, much like a DJ's opening track that gets everyone on the dance floor.

2. Tell Your Story: Share your professional journey, including your motivations and what led you to your current role. This narrative can help create a personal connection with your audience.

3. Highlight Key Achievements: Include specific accomplishments that demonstrate your expertise and value. Just as a DJ might highlight their most memorable performances, you should showcase your successes to build credibility.

4. Include a Call to Action: Encourage readers to connect with you or visit your website. This is like a DJ inviting the crowd to join them on the dance floor for an unforgettable experience.

5. Keep It Concise and Clear: While it's important to share your story, ensure that your About section remains focused and easy to read. Avoid overwhelming your audience with too much information, just as a DJ avoids playing too many songs at once to maintain the energy of the party.

The About section on LinkedIn™ is a vital component of your professional profile, serving as a platform to showcase your personality, expertise, and unique value. By crafting an engaging and authentic About section, you can make a lasting impression, build trust, and encourage meaningful connections. Just as a disco ball reflects light and energy throughout a party, your About section can illuminate your professional journey and draw people into your network. Embrace this opportunity to shine, and watch as your LinkedIn™ presence transforms into a vibrant hub of engagement and opportunity.

ABOUT SECTION

Template for an About Section

Are you a:

EXAMPLE

[Emoji] [Target audience 1]?

[Emoji] [Target audience 2]?

[Emoji] [Target audience 3]?

🏃 *Event organiser looking for something unique?*

🎉 *Corporate team building coordinator?*

🎂 *Birthday celebrant wanting an unforgettable bash?*

Do you feel:

[Emoji] [Pain point 1]

[Emoji] [Pain point 2]

[Emoji] [Pain point 3]

[Emoji] [Pain point 4]

[Emoji] [Pain point 5]

● *Overwhelmed by party planning details?*

● *Unsure how to create a truly memorable event?*

💸 *Worried about blowing your budget?*

🎵 *Confused about choosing the right music?*

🎤 *Concerned about keeping all guests entertained?*

If so I can help.

I have taken everything I have
learned over the past [X] years,
from [experience range].

*I have taken everything I have learned over the
past 15 years, from planning intimate
gatherings to large-scale corporate events*

[Emoji] [Key achievement 1].

[Emoji] [Key achievement 2]

[Emoji] [Key achievement 3]

[Emoji] [Key achievement 4].

🏆 *Organised a large charity disco ball, raising £10K*

🎆 *Planned celebrity-attended themed parties*

🏅 *Won 'Best Event Planner' award three times*

● *Coordinated disco-themed events*

How can I help you?

[Brief description of how you
help clients]

*I transform your vision into a dazzling disco reality,
handling everything from venue selection to the last
song of the night, ensuring your event is talked
about for years to come.*

What we offer:

[Emoji] [Service 1]

[Emoji] [Service 2]

[Emoji] [Service 3]

[Emoji] [Service 4]

🎵 *Curated disco playlists tailored to your audience*

💡 *Stunning light shows and disco ball installations*

🍸 *Themed catering and signature cocktail creation*

🕺 *Live performers and DJs specialising in disco*

Let's chat: [Emoji] [Contact method] *Let's chat:* ✉ *boogie@discopartyplanner.com*

A

CHOICE POINTS

If you want to learn more about your personal profile, turn to page 121.
If you're interested in content strategy, turn to page 34.
To explore 'All-Star' profile, see page 8.

TOP TIP

The most important thing is to make your About section stand out by infusing your personality and unique perspective into the narrative. If your About section is engaging and authentic, it will draw people in and make them want to learn more about you.

2. ALGORITHM

A

Imagine you're at the biggest party in town, filled with colourful confetti, lively music, and a dazzling disco ball spinning above. This party represents LinkedIn™, a vibrant space where people connect and share ideas.

As you navigate through the party, you're looking for the most exciting activities and interesting people to meet. Here's how it works:

Relevance

Just like you'd seek out games or conversations that interest you at a party, LinkedIn™ shows you posts and profiles that align with your professional interests and goals. If you're passionate about marketing, for instance, LinkedIn™ will highlight content related to marketing trends and tips.

Engagement

Picture some party areas buzzing with energy, filled with laughter and conversation. You'd naturally gravitate toward those lively spots, right? LinkedIn™ operates similarly. It prioritises posts that have received a lot of likes, comments, and shares, indicating they're popular and engaging. The more people interact with a post, the more likely it is to catch your attention.

Connections

At a party, you often want to find friends or meet new people through mutual acquaintances. LinkedIn™ pays attention to your connections and what they engage with. If your connections are enjoying a particular post, LinkedIn™ assumes you might find it interesting too, helping you discover content through your network.

Freshness

Imagine someone announcing a new game or activity at the party - you'd want to check it out immediately. Similarly, LinkedIn™ values fresh content; it considers how recent a post is when deciding what to show you, ensuring you're always in the loop with the latest updates and discussions.

As you explore the LinkedIn™ party, the platform's algorithm acts like a helpful host, guiding you to the most relevant conversations and introducing you to intriguing people. Sometimes, you'll find exactly what you're looking for right away, while other times you might need to explore a bit to uncover hidden gems.

A

ALGORITHM

Just like in any social setting, the more you engage and participate on LinkedIn™, the more rewarding your experience will be, opening doors to new opportunities and connections.

CHOICE POINTS

If you want to learn more about engagement, turn to page 46.
If you're interested in data insights, go to page 40.
To explore keywords, it's page 83.

TOP TIP

The key to mastering the LinkedIn®
algorithm is consistent, high-
quality engagement. Think of it as
being the life of the party, the more
you interact genuinely with others'
content, the more the algorithm
will favour your own posts.
Regular, meaningful comments
and shares are like your best dance
moves, keeping you in the spotlight
of the LinkedIn® disco.

A

3. 'ALL-STAR' PROFILE

Imagine you're at a spectacular party, where some guests really stand out. These standout guests are like the all-star profiles on LinkedIn™.

An all-star profile on LinkedIn™ is like one of these standout guests at the party. It's a profile that's been meticulously crafted to showcase someone's skills, experiences, and achievements in the best possible light. Just as these standout guests are dressed to impress and know how to make a great impression, an all-star profile is complete with a professional photo, a compelling headline, a detailed summary, and a thorough list of skills and experiences.

Having an all-star profile on LinkedIn™ is important for several reasons:

Visibility
Just as standout guests catch everyone's eye at the party, an all-star profile stands out to potential clients and other professionals on LinkedIn™. It increases your visibility and makes it easier for people to find you when they're searching for someone with your skills and expertise.

Credibility
Much like how standout guests imply high quality and attention to detail, an all-star profile signals to others that you're serious about your professional presence on LinkedIn™. It adds credibility to your personal brand and makes you more attractive to potential customers or business partners.

Networking
Just as people might be drawn to the VIP guests at a party, an all-star profile can attract more connections and networking opportunities on LinkedIn™. When your profile is well-optimised, it's more likely to spark interest and initiate conversations with other professionals in your industry. A well-optimised LinkedIn™ profile is a complete, professional, and up-to-date profile that showcases your skills, experience, and accomplishments.

Business Opportunities
Similar to how standout guests might receive compliments and invitations to other events, an all-star profile can open doors to exciting business opportunities, such as collaboration offers, speaking engagements, and more.

A

ALL-STAR PROFILE

To achieve all-star status on LinkedIn™, you need to ensure your profile is 100% complete. Here are the key components:

1. Professional Profile Picture: A clear, professional headshot where you appear approachable and authentic.

2. Compelling Headline: A headline that captures your unique value and includes relevant keywords.

3. About section: An engaging summary that introduces you, showcases your personality, and highlights your professional journey.

4. Experience Section: A comprehensive list of your career history with specific descriptions of your roles and achievements.

5. Skills: At least five skills that highlight your strengths.

6. Industry and Location: Updated information to enhance your profile's visibility.

7. Education: Listing your qualifications to connect with fellow alumni and increase discoverability.

8. Connections: Aim for at least 50 connections to achieve all-star status.

By having an all-star profile on LinkedIn™, you become one of those standout guests at the party – more visible, credible, and attractive to others in your professional network, ultimately helping you advance your business goals.

CHOICE POINTS

If you want to learn more about your personal profile, turn to page 121.
If you're interested in goal setting, turn to page 208.
To explore optimisation, go to page 117.

A

4. ANALYTICS

Imagine you're hosting an amazing party, complete with a variety of activities, from dancing to games. Every day, you want to know which activities are the most popular and why.

Analytics at the party is like keeping track of which activities the guests enjoy the most and understanding the reasons behind their preferences. Here's how it works:

Data
Just as you would keep track of how many guests participate in each activity, analytics collects data on various activities on LinkedIn™. For example, it tracks how many people visit your LinkedIn™ profile, how many likes and comments your posts receive, and how many new connections you make.

Patterns and Trends
By analysing your party data, you can identify patterns and trends. For instance, you might notice that the dance floor is packed in the evening, while the games area is more popular in the afternoon. Similarly, LinkedIn™ analytics can help you identify trends in your activity, such as the best times to post content or the types of posts that generate the most engagement.

Insights
Understanding these patterns and trends gives you valuable insights into your party planning. You might realise that you need to arrange more dance sessions in the evening to meet demand, or that you should introduce new games based on your guests' preferences. Similarly, LinkedIn™ analytics provides insights into your presence on the platform, helping you understand what resonates with your audience and how to optimise your profile and content for better results.

Decision-Making
Armed with these insights, you can make informed decisions to improve your party. You might adjust the schedule, introduce new activities, or invest more in promoting certain events. Likewise, on LinkedIn™, analytics empower you to make strategic decisions about your networking and content strategy to achieve your goals, whether it's growing your business or establishing yourself as a thought leader in your industry.

By using analytics, you can ensure that your LinkedIn™ presence is as successful and engaging as your party, attracting the right people and making the most of every opportunity.

A

CHOICE POINTS

If you want to learn more about strategy, turn to page 165.
If you're interested in data insights, turn to page 40.
To explore the algorithm, go to page 6.

TOP TIP

When it comes to LinkedIn®
analytics, the most important
thing is to remember that you
can't measure everything, so
focus on one key metric that will
truly move the dial for your
business. Whether it's
engagement, profile views, or
connection growth, identifying
that one metric is key.

A

5. ARTICLES

Imagine your disco party has a stage where you can showcase your best performances and share your expertise with the crowd. LinkedIn™ articles are just like that stage, they give you a platform to demonstrate your knowledge and establish yourself as a thought leader in your industry.

Why Are LinkedIn® Articles Important?

Establish Expertise
Articles allow you to dive deep into topics, showcasing your knowledge and experience. It's like performing an extended set at your party, demonstrating your range and skill as a DJ.

Increase Visibility
Well-written articles can be shared widely, increasing your visibility beyond your immediate network. This is similar to how a standout performance at your party might get people talking and attract more guests.

Engage Your Network
Articles provide a way to start meaningful conversations with your connections. It's like sparking discussions among partygoers about the music you're playing.

SEO Benefits
LinkedIn™ articles can appear in search engine results, potentially attracting new connections. This is akin to your party being featured in local event listings, drawing in more attendees.

How to Create Effective LinkedIn® Articles

1.*Choose Relevant Topics:* Write about subjects that matter to your target audience. It's like selecting the perfect playlist that resonates with your party crowd.

2.*Use Engaging Headlines:* Craft attention-grabbing titles to entice readers. This is similar to announcing an exciting upcoming track to keep the dance floor full.

3.*Include Visual Elements:* Incorporate images, infographics, or videos to make your articles more engaging. It's like adding visual effects to your DJ set to enhance the experience.

4. Keep It Concise and Structured: Use clear headings and bullet points to make your article easy to read. This is akin to organizing your music into well-defined sets for easy listening.

5. End with a Call-to-Action: Encourage readers to engage by commenting, sharing, or connecting with you. It's like inviting partygoers to request songs or join you on the dance floor.

Frequency and Timing

While there's no strict rule, aim to publish articles consistently, perhaps once or twice a month. This regular cadence keeps your audience engaged, much like hosting regular themed nights at your disco to keep guests coming back.

LinkedIn™ articles are your opportunity to take centre stage and showcase your professional expertise. By creating valuable, engaging content, you can establish yourself as a thought leader, increase your visibility, and foster meaningful connections within your industry. So, step up to the microphone and let your professional voice be heard through compelling LinkedIn™ articles.

Top Tips for Creating a LinkedIn® Article: Let's Get This Party Started!

Creating a LinkedIn™ article is like throwing a fabulous disco party; everyone wants to join in, but you need to set the right mood! Here are some top tips to ensure your article shines like a disco ball:

Article Length: Find Your Groove

Aim for articles between 1,500 and 2,000 words to keep the dance floor buzzing. Just like a great DJ knows when to drop the beat, you should know when to keep it concise. If you can deliver your message in fewer words, go for it, clarity is key.

Use of External Links: Sparkle with Credibility

Do sprinkle in some external links. Just like the reflections from a disco ball, these links can enhance your article's shine by referencing authoritative sources or providing extra insights. Make sure they're relevant and add value, so your readers feel like they're getting the VIP treatment.

A

ARTICLES

Author Bio: Introduce the Star of the Show

Wrap up your article with a brief author bio that introduces you as the star of the party. This not only establishes your credibility but also helps readers understand your background and expertise. Don't forget to link to your LinkedIn™ profile, so they can keep the connection going!

Avoiding Duplicate Content: Keep It Fresh on the Dance Floor

Distinctive Content: Just like every great party needs its own unique vibe, your LinkedIn™ articles should offer fresh insights that differ from your blog posts or other online content. Duplicate content can dull your sparkle and confuse your audience.

SEO Implications: When similar content appears across multiple platforms, search engines struggle to determine which version is the life of the party. This can lead to lower visibility for all versions, meaning your valuable insights might get lost in the crowd. By providing original content on LinkedIn™, you increase the chances of your article shining brighter in search results.

DID YOU KNOW?

Only 0.1% of LinkedIn® users have published an article? This presents a significant opportunity for businesses to establish themselves as thought leaders.

A

ARTICLES

Audience Engagement: Your LinkedIn™ audience is like a different crowd on the dance floor. Crafting unique content tailored to their interests and challenges fosters deeper engagement and lively discussions. This approach helps you connect more effectively with professionals who are specifically looking for insights relevant to their industry or role.

Building Authority: Original content helps establish you as the disco ball of your field, reflecting knowledge and expertise. When you share unique insights and experiences, you position yourself as a thought leader, which can lead to increased credibility and exciting opportunities within your network.

CHOICE POINTS

If you want to learn more about posts, turn to page 127.
If you're interested in thought leadership, turn to page 182.
• To explore collaborative articles, go to page 24.

TOP TIP

By understanding the importance of crafting compelling articles and leveraging user engagement strategies, businesses can enhance their visibility, establish credibility, and connect with their target audience effectively. The key takeaway is that while only a small percentage of users create content, the potential for impact is substantial for those who do.

B

6. BANNER

At the party the first thing your guests see as they arrive is a stunning entrance decorated with lights, balloons, and a welcoming sign. This entrance sets the tone for the entire event and gives your guests a glimpse of what to expect.

The banner on your LinkedIn™ profile serves a similar purpose. It's the large image at the top of your profile that helps to convey your personal brand, professional identity, and what you're all about. Here's how it works:

Brand Identity

Just as the entrance decor reflects the theme and vibe of your party, the banner on your LinkedIn™ profile should reflect who you are as a professional. It's an opportunity to showcase your personality, expertise, and interests. For instance, if you're in the tech industry, your banner might feature sleek, modern designs, or images related to technology.

Visual Impact

Like a striking party entrance that catches the eye of your guests, your LinkedIn™ banner should make a visual impact and grab the attention of visitors to your profile. It should be visually appealing and relevant to your industry or profession. A well-designed banner can make your profile stand out and leave a lasting impression.

Professionalism

While you want your banner to be eye-catching, it should also convey professionalism and credibility. Avoid using overly flashy or distracting images that may detract from your professional image. Think of it as setting the right tone for your guests; you want them to be impressed but also understand the seriousness of the event.

Consistency

Your banner should be consistent with your personal brand and the rest of your LinkedIn™ profile. It should complement your profile photo, headline, and summary to create a cohesive and memorable impression. Just like a well-coordinated party entrance, everything should work together to tell a unified story.

Practical Tips

When creating your banner, consider featuring images or graphics that represent your industry, showcase your work, or highlight your achievements. Here are some practical tips:

B

BANNER

1. Dimensions: The recommended dimensions for the LinkedIn™ banner are 1584 pixels wide by 396 pixels tall.
2. Tools: Use a tool like Canva to design your banner. Canva offers a variety of templates that you can customise to fit your brand.
3. Content Ideas: You can include images of yourself at work, your company logo, or even a quote that resonates with your professional ethos.
4. Consistency: Ensure that the colours and style of your banner align with your overall branding and professional image.
5. Contact information: Make it easy for connections to get in touch with you.

Frequency of Change
As for how often you should change your LinkedIn™ banner, it depends on your personal preference and circumstances. If you have a specific event, promotion, or milestone that you want to highlight, you might change your banner more frequently. Otherwise, you can change it periodically to keep your profile fresh and relevant.

By paying attention to your LinkedIn™ banner, you ensure that the first impression visitors get is as impressive and inviting as the entrance to your party, setting the stage for meaningful connections and professional opportunities.

Overall, the banner behind your LinkedIn™ profile is a valuable opportunity to make a memorable impression and communicate your personal brand to visitors. Take the time to create a banner that reflects who you are as a professional and engages your audience effectively.

CHOICE POINTS

If you want to learn more about images, turn to page 72.
If you're interested in exploring your unique value proposition, turn to page 188.
To explore building your brand, go to page 21.

B

7. BELL NOTIFICATION

At the party you may have some loyal guests who love to know when you've organised new activities or special events. They don't want to keep checking in or wandering around the venue every day to find out what's happening.

That's where the notification bell on LinkedIn™ comes in! It's like having a little bell at the entrance of your party that your loyal guests can ring to be notified whenever you make a new post or share exciting updates. Here's how it works:

Location
The notification bell is conveniently placed right under the banner image on your LinkedIn™ profile, both on your personal profile and on your company page.

Notification Options
When your guests click on the bell, they have two options: a filled-in grey bell or just the outline of a bell. If they choose the filled-in grey bell, it's like saying, "Yes, p.ease notify me about every activity you organise!" If they opt for just the outline, it means, "I only want to know about the most popular activities."

You do not get a notification if someone has turned your notification bell on or off.

Think of the notification bell on LnkedIn™ as your personal party alert system It's a handy way for your guests to stay updated with your latest activities and for you to keep track of what your favourite guests are up to without having to scroll through your entire feed.

Encouraging your connections to ring the bell on your profile ensures they never miss out on your latest posts or special offers; it helps maintain engagement and keeps you top of mind in their professional network. So, just ask them to ring the bell, and watch as your interactions flourish.

B

BELL NOTIFICATION

Benefits for Business Owners and Leaders

Stay Informed: By activating notifications for your key prospects, you can keep up with their activities and insights. This allows you to engage meaningfully with their content just as a DJ interacts with the crowd to maintain the party's energy. A LinkedIn™ prospect is a person or organisation that has the potential to become a customer for your product or service.

Engage with Content: When you see that a prospect has posted something, you can comment or share your thoughts, fostering a deeper connection. This engagement is just like joining the dance floor and showing off your moves, making you more visible and memorable to your audience.

Build Relationships: Regularly interacting with your prospects' posts helps to build rapport and trust. Just as a DJ builds a connection with their audience through music, your engagement can create a sense of familiarity and goodwill.

Identify Opportunities: By staying updated on your prospects' posts, you can identify potential opportunities for collaboration or business. This is like spotting a chance to collaborate with another artist at the party, leading to exciting new ventures.

Enhance Your Visibility: When you engage with your prospects' content, you not only increase your visibility to them but also to their connections. This ripple effect can expand your network, similar to how a great party attracts more guests as word spreads.

CHOICE POINTS

If you want to learn more privacy settings, turn to page 131.
To explore more about notifications, turn to page 110.
If you are interested in lead generation, go to page 89.

B

8. BUILD YOUR BRAND

Imagine you're not just hosting parties, but you're now the owner of a renowned event-planning company known for its unique themes and exceptional guest experiences. Here's how you can build your event-planning brand on LinkedIn™ and treat your profile like a sales page:

Craft Your Brand Story (The Party Narrative)
Just as you would have a compelling story behind your event-planning business, share your journey on your LinkedIn™ profile. Talk about how your passion for creating memorable experiences began, the inspiration behind your unique party themes, and the values that drive your business. This sets the stage for your brand identity.

Showcase Your Best Events (Highlight Your Services)
Your LinkedIn™ profile is like a photo album of your most successful parties. Feature your top services prominently in your profile, highlighting their unique selling points and benefits. Use rich media, such as images or videos, to showcase your events and entice potential clients.

Engage with Your Party Guests (Build Relationships)
Engage with your LinkedIn™ connections just like you would with guests at your events. Respond to comments on your posts, join industry conversations, and reach out to connect with like-minded professionals. Building genuine relationships fosters trust and loyalty, essential for a successful event-planning business.

Share Your Party Planning Secrets (Demonstrate Expertise)
Position yourself as a thought leader in the event-planning industry by sharing valuable insights, tips, and expertise on LinkedIn™. Write articles, share industry news, or offer advice related to event planning. Establishing yourself as an authority builds credibility and attracts followers eager to learn from you.

Offer a Party Favour (Call-to-Action)
Just like you might offer a party favour to guests, include a call-to-action on your LinkedIn™ profile to encourage engagement or lead generation. This could be inviting people to visit your website, sign up for a newsletter, or schedule a consultation. Make it easy for potential clients to take the next step in their journey with your brand.

B

BUILD YOUR BRAND

Measure Your Party Success (Track Your Success)
Finally, keep track of your LinkedIn™ performance metrics to gauge the effectiveness of your brand-building efforts. Monitor metrics such as profile views, engagement on posts, and connection growth. Use these insights to refine your strategy and continue growing your event-planning brand on LinkedIn™.

By following these steps, you can effectively build your brand on LinkedIn™ and leverage your profile as a powerful sales page to attract, engage, and convert potential clients into loyal fans of your event-planning business.

Remember, just like planning a great party, building your brand on LinkedIn™ takes time, creativity, and consistent effort. Keep refining your approach based on what resonates with your audience, and don't be afraid to let your unique personality shine through.

CHOICE POINTS

If you want to learn more about engagement, turn to page 48.
To explore more about analytics, turn to page 12.
To find out about name pronunciation, go to page 99.

DID YOU KNOW?
As at August 2024 there are 67 million companies listed on LinkedIn®?

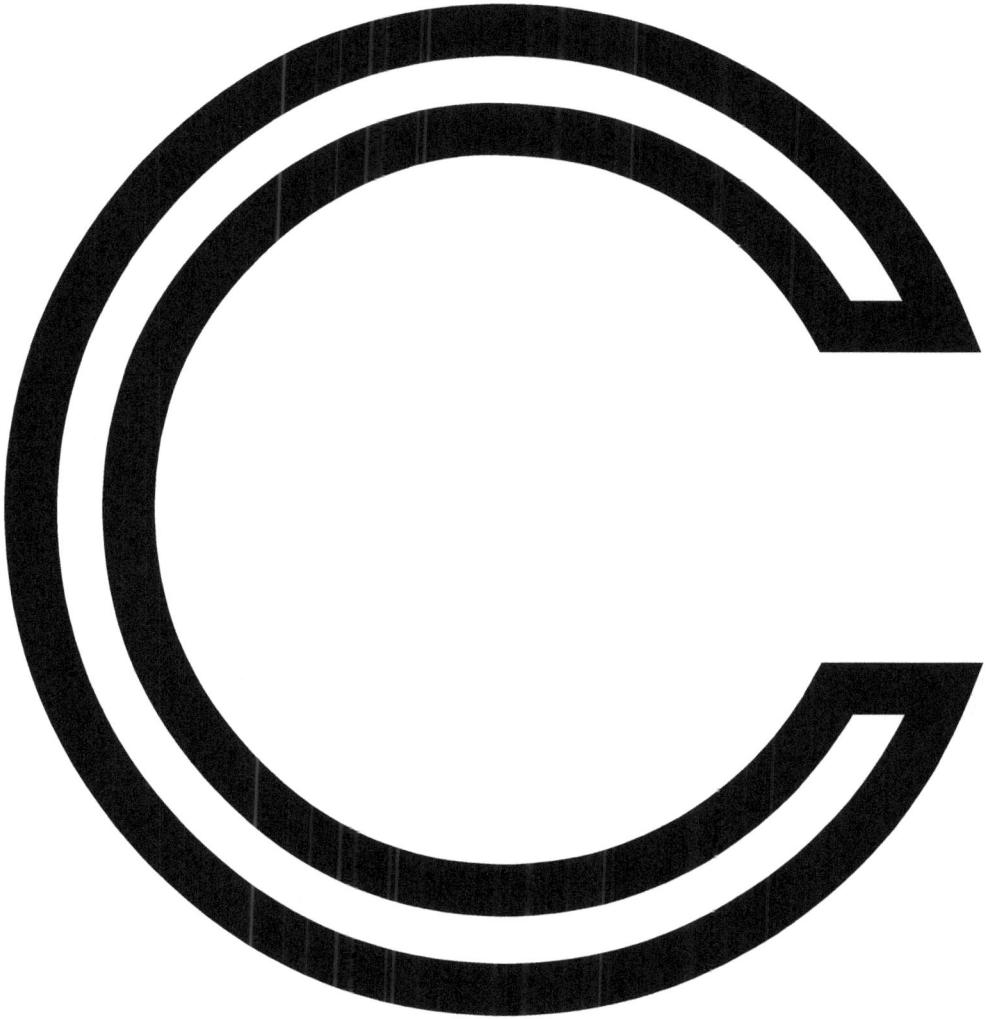

9. COLLABORATIVE ARTICLES

Think about your disco party where everyone is having a blast, dancing, and sharing ideas about the best music and moves. Now imagine if you could gather some of your friends to create a fantastic dance routine together, combining everyone's unique styles and talents. That's what collaborative articles on LinkedIn™ are all about; a chance to work together and share knowledge. Here's how it works:

Working Together
Collaborative articles allow multiple professionals to contribute their insights and expertise on a specific topic. It's like bringing together a group of talented dancers to create an amazing performance. Each person adds their unique flair, making the final product even better than if one person did it alone.

Sharing Knowledge
By collaborating on articles, you can share valuable information and tips with a wider audience. This is like having your friends at the party share their best dance moves with everyone, helping everyone learn and improve. When you contribute to a collaborative article, you're not just sharing your knowledge, you're also learning from others.

Building Connections
Participating in collaborative articles helps you connect with other professionals in your industry. Just as dancing with different people at your party can lead to new friendships, working together on articles allows you to network and build relationships with fellow contributors. These connections can lead to future collaborations or opportunities.

Increasing Visibility
When you contribute to a collaborative article, you gain visibility among a broader audience. It's like having your dance routine showcased at a big event, where more people can see your talent. This increased exposure can help you attract new followers, clients, and connections on LinkedIn™.

Advantages

1. Enhanced Credibility
Contributing to collaborative articles boosts your credibility as an expert in your field. Just like being part of a well choreographed dance routine makes you look good, being featured in a collaborative article shows that others value your insights and expertise.

C

COLLABORATIVE ARTICLES

2. Diverse Perspectives
Collaborative articles bring together different viewpoints and experiences. It's like mixing various dance styles to create a unique performance that appeals to a wider audience. This diversity enriches the content and makes it more engaging for readers.

3. Opportunity for Learning
Working with others on articles provides a chance to learn new things. Just as you might pick up new dance moves from your friends, collaborating allows you to gain insights and knowledge from your fellow contributors, enhancing your own skills and understanding.

How to get a badge
LinkedIn™'s Community Top Voice badge is a light gold badge that appears under a user's profile headline to recognise members who contribute significantly to collaborative articles.
The badge is awarded based on a user's active participation and the skills they showcase in specific topics. Users can earn the badge by being one of the most upvoted contributors to collaborative articles for a particular skill.
To be eligible, users must contribute at least three times within the same skill, but that doesn't guarantee you'll receive a badge. Some skills may have more contributors than others, making it more difficult to earn a badge.
Badges are temporary and last 60 days, and they can be revoked if a user violates LinkedIn™'s professional conduct policies.

Collaborative articles on LinkedIn™ are like creating an incredible dance routine with friends at your disco party. By working together, sharing knowledge, and building connections, you can create something truly special that showcases everyone's talents. So, get ready to join forces with other professionals, contribute to collaborative articles, and let your expertise shine on LinkedIn™.

CHOICE POINTS

If you want to learn more about articles, turn to page 12.
To explore more about thought leadership, turn to page 182.
To find out about trending topics, go to page 184.

10. COMPANY PAGES

Let's talk about Company Pages. Your event-planning business grows, and you decide to open a dedicated venue for hosting events. This venue is like a Company Page on LinkedIn™. It's a place where people can learn all about your event-planning business, even if they don't know you personally. Here's how it works:

The Entrance

Just like your venue has a grand entrance where people can see the beautiful decorations and themes you offer, a Company Page has a profile picture and banner that showcase what your business is all about. It's like the sign outside your venue that tells people they've arrived at the right place for unforgettable events.

The Event Menu

Your venue has a menu that lists all the different types of events you can organise, from weddings to corporate gatherings. Similarly, a Company Page on LinkedIn™ showcases what your business does, its services, and any special promotions or events. It's like a virtual menu for visitors to explore.

The Story

Remember how you share stories about your event-planning adventures on your personal profile? On your Company Page, you can share the story of how your business started, the talented team behind the scenes, and why your events are the best. This connection helps potential clients feel a part of your event-loving community.

Personal Profile vs. Company Page

What's the difference between your personal profile and your Company Page?
Your personal profile is all about you – your stories, your experiences, and your passion for event planning. Your Company Page is about your business as a whole – what you offer, how you create memorable experiences, and why clients should choose your services over others.

A Company Page on LinkedIn™ is like a virtual venue for your event-planning business, where people can learn all about what you do and why you excel in your field. It's a place to showcase your brand, connect with clients, and spread the love for unforgettable events far and wide.

COMPANY PAGES
Components of a LinkedIn™ Company Page

People Section
The People section showcases your employees, like being introduced to the talented dancers on the floor. It allows visitors to see who's behind the brand, highlighting your team's expertise and culture, and creating a sense of community.

Careers Page
This is your invitation for potential employees to join the party. The Careers Page offers job postings and insights into your company culture, attracting talent who want to be part of your vibrant team.

Showcase Pages
Like themed areas at a disco, Showcase Pages allow you to highlight specific products, services, or initiatives. This targeted approach helps you cater to different audience segments and promote various aspects of your business.

Location
Your company's physical address is essential for helping potential clients and employees find you, much like having clear directions to the party venue. You can even add multiple locations if applicable.

Page Analytics
Just as a DJ monitors the crowd's reaction to adjust their set, LinkedIn™ provides analytics to track your page's performance. Insights into follower growth, engagement metrics, and post reach help refine your strategy.

A well-structured LinkedIn™ Company Page is essential for building your brand, engaging with your audience, and attracting potential clients and employees. Much like a vibrant disco party that draws in guests and keeps them entertained.

CHOICE POINTS

If you want to learn more about competitor analysis, turn to page 28.
To explore more about employee advocacy, go to page 43.
To learn about building a brand, turn to page 21.

C

11. COMPETITOR ANALYSIS

Your company's LinkedIn™ page is like your exclusive VIP lounge, where you showcase your best moves and attract party-goers. But just as in any vibrant nightlife scene, there are other hot spots vying for attention.

In this bustling LinkedIn™ disco, each event-planning company has set up its own unique dance floor (Company Page), complete with dazzling lights (updates) and a guest list of event enthusiasts. But how do you know if your party is the talk of the town?

This is where LinkedIn™'s competitor analysis comes in handy. It's like having a secret peek at the other venues' guest books and playlists. You can see how many revellers are visiting each competitor's party (page views) and how often they're dropping new tracks (post frequency). Best of all, you get to choose which rival parties you want to measure yourself against, allowing you to ensure your disco remains the hottest ticket in town.

By keeping an eye on the competition, you can fine-tune your own party strategy, making sure your LinkedIn™ presence keeps the professional crowd grooving to your beat.

Checking Clients
Just like you'd want to know how many people visit each business on LinkedIn™, you can see how many followers each company's page has. More followers mean more people are interested in what that company is doing.

Counting Events
Each event-planning company also shares updates, like new event themes or special deals. On LinkedIn™, you can see how many updates each company posts. More updates mean the company is active and engaging with clients.

Learning from Others
By looking at how other businesses are doing, you can learn from their success and get ideas for your own business. If a competitor has more followers, maybe you could try some of their strategies to attract more clients to your business. It helps you learn from them and improve your own business's performance.

C

COMPETITOR ANALYSIS

How to Conduct Competitor Analysis on LinkedIn®

1. **Identify Competitors:** Start by identifying your direct and indirect competitors. Direct competitors offer similar services, while indirect competitors might offer complementary services that could attract your target audience.
2. **Track Followers:** Monitor the number of followers on your competitors' Company Pages. This gives you an idea of their reach and popularity.
3. **Analyse Content:** Look at the type and frequency of content your competitor's post. Pay attention to what gets the most engagement (likes, comments, shares). This can give you insights into what your audience might find interesting.
4. **Engagement Metrics:** Evaluate how engaged their audience is. High engagement rates can indicate strong customer loyalty and interest.
5. **Benchmarking:** Use LinkedIn™'s tools to benchmark your Company Page against your competitors. This can help you identify areas where you excel and areas that need improvement.

By conducting regular competitor analysis on LinkedIn™, you can stay ahead of the competition, refine your strategies, and ensure your business continues to attract and delight clients.

CHOICE POINTS

If you want to learn more about company pages, turn to page 26.

To explore more about analytics, turn to page 10.

To find out about the bell notification, go to page 19.

TOP TIP

Make sure to activate the bell notification for your competitors' Company Pages. You'll not only keep your finger on the pulse of the competition but also position yourself to react quickly and effectively, making sure your LinkedIn® presence remains the life of the party.

12. CONNECTION NOTE

When you want to invite someone to one of your fabulous events, you can write a little note to go with the invitation. Think of it like adding a personal touch to your party invitation before sending it out.

On LinkedIn™, when you want to connect with someone, you have the option to send a message along with your invitation.

But here's the twist: you only have a limited space to work with, just like fitting all your exciting event details onto a small invitation card. LinkedIn™ gives you 300 characters, so you need to be concise yet compelling.

Here are some tips for crafting an effective connection note:

1. Personalise: Mention how you know the person or why you want to connect. For example: 'I loved your recent post about innovative event themes!'

2. Be Specific: Explain why you're reaching out: 'I'd love to discuss potential collaboration on corporate events.'

3. Add Value: Offer something of interest to them: 'I have some unique insights on sustainable event planning I'd like to share.'

4. Keep it Brief: Remember, you only have 300 characters. Make every word count.

5. Be Professional: While friendly, maintain a professional tone appropriate for LinkedIn™.

6. Call to Action: End with a clear next step: 'Would you be open to a quick chat about our next event?'

Your connection note is like your party invitation - it should be enticing, clear, and make the recipient excited to connect with you. Just as you'd tailor each party invitation to the guest, customise each connection note to the individual you're reaching out to on LinkedIn™.

CONNECTION NOTE

CHOICE POINTS

If you want to learn more about direct messaging, turn to page 42.
To explore more about who's viewed your profile, turn to page 201.
To find out about finding leads, go to page 55.

DID YOU KNOW?

LinkedIn® limits the number of personalised connection notes that basic account holders can send per month to five to combat spammy sales notes.

TOP TIP

Once a connection request is accepted, send a personalised message to start a conversation. Approach connections with authenticity and value, just as you would aim to make real connections at a networking event or party

13. CONNECTIONS

At your event-planning company, you host exclusive preview parties for upcoming event themes. There are two types of guests: those with a special invitation to join the party inside your venue, and those who can observe from outside through the windows.

Connections (Invited Guests): These are like the guests who have received a personal invitation to join the preview party inside your venue. They're loyal clients whom you know, like and trust. Just like connections on LinkedIn™, they have access to everything happening inside your venue – they can see your latest event designs, chat with you, and even experience the themed activities first-hand.

Followers (Observers through the Window): Followers, on the other hand, are like the curious passers-by who stop to watch the preview party from outside your venue. They're interested in what you're doing, but they're not part of the exclusive gathering. Similarly, followers on LinkedIn™ can see your posts and updates, but they're not directly connected to you. They can't chat with you or see your private information like your connections can.

Both connections and followers can appreciate your event-planning expertise, but connections have a closer relationship with you, like a two-way conversation, whilst followers are more like observers enjoying the view through the window.

Key differences between connections and followers on LinkedIn®:

1. Access: Connections have full access to your profile, including contact information and detailed work history. Followers can only see public information.

2. Interaction: You can message connections directly, but not followers (unless they've allowed it in their settings).

3. Notifications: You receive notifications about your connections' activities, such as job changes or work anniversaries. You don't receive these for followers.

4. Network Visibility: Your connections can see your network (unless you've changed your settings), but followers cannot.

5. Content Reach: While both connections and followers can see your posts, content shared with connections often gets more visibility in their feeds.

C

CONNECTIONS

6. Endorsements and Recommendations: Only connections can endorse your skills or write reccmmendations for you.

Building a network of quality connections is crucial for maximising your LinkedIn™ presence, much like curating an exclusive guest list for the ultimate disco party. You want to invite individuals who will not only enjoy the vibe but also contribute to the energy on the dance floor. However having followers can also be beneficial, just like having a lively crowd that adds to the atmosphere, especially if you're aiming to establish thought leadership in your industry.

Think of your followers as the enthusiastic party-goers who may not be on your VIP list but are still eager to join in on the fun and share your message with others. Strive for a balance that aligns with your professional goals, just as a DJ balances popular hits with unique tracks to keep the crowd engaged. By cultivating meaningful connections while also growing your follower base, you can create a thriving LinkedIn™ presence that resonates with your audience and keeps the professional party going strong.

CHOICE POINTS

If you want to learn more about connection notes, turn to page 30.
To explore more about followers, turn to page 57.
To check out privacy settings, go to page 131.

TOP TIP

When it comes to building your network on LinkedIn®, remember that you don't need to connect with everyone; focus on being strategic. Invite only those who will add value to your professional network.

14. CONTENT STRATEGY

Imagine LinkedIn™ as a bustling disco party where every business is vying for attention on the dance floor. A content strategy is your carefully choreographed dance routine that helps you stand out from the crowd and win the spotlight. Here's why a content strategy is crucial for winning business:

Builds Brand Awareness
A well-executed content strategy helps increase visibility and awareness of your business among your target audience. By consistently sharing engaging content, you can attract new clients, keep existing ones excited, and differentiate your event-planning services from competitors. Think of it as decorating your party venue with vibrant colours and lights that draw people in.

Drives Customer Engagement
Engaging content fosters interaction and dialogue with your audience, building meaningful relationships and client loyalty. By providing value, inspiration, and entertainment through your posts, you can deepen connections with your clients and keep them coming back for more, just like a dance floor that keeps guests moving and grooving all night long.

Establishes Authority and Trust
Sharing informative and educational content positions your business as a trusted authority in the event-planning industry. By demonstrating your expertise, creativity, and commitment to quality through your content, you instil confidence and trust in your brand, making it more likely for clients to choose your services over others. It's like being the DJ who knows exactly how to keep the party going with the right tunes.

Generates Leads and Sales
A strategic content strategy can drive traffic to your business, generate leads, and ultimately increase sales. By showcasing your events, highlighting client successes, and providing incentives for engagement, you can convert followers into clients and drive business growth. Just as a well-promoted party attracts a crowd, effective content can fill your calendar with events.

C

CONTENT STRATEGY

A Content Strategy Outline on LinkedIn®:

1. Identify Your Target Audience

Determine who your ideal clients are. Are they corporate businesses looking for team-building events, couples planning weddings, or perhaps organisations hosting charity galas? Understanding your audience will help tailor your content to their interests and needs.

2. Define Brand Voice and Messaging

Establish a consistent brand voice that reflects the personality of your business. Are you fun and energetic, sophisticated and classy, or innovative and trendy? Define your messaging pillars, such as creative themes, flawless execution, or personalised service to communicate your unique value proposition.

3. Create Engaging Content

Develop a variety of content types to showcase your event planning expertise and engage your audience. This could include:

Event Showcases: Highlight your latest events, themed parties, and signature concepts. Share stunning photos and descriptions to inspire potential clients.

Behind-the-Scenes: Take your audience behind the scenes of event preparation. Share stories about your planning process, introduce your team members, and offer glimpses into your creative brainstorming sessions to build authenticity and trust.

Client Testimonials: Feature testimonials and reviews from satisfied clients to build credibility and social proof. Share their experiences and feedback to showcase the quality and satisfaction of your events.

CONTENT STRATEGY

<u>Event-Planning Tips:</u> Share helpful planning tips, tricks, and trends to engage your audience and position your business as an authority. Offer checklists, how-to guides, and insider secrets to educate and inspire your followers.

<u>Industry Insights:</u> Share your thoughts on industry trends, emerging technologies in event planning, and predictions for the future of events.

4. Optimise for LinkedIn™

Tailor your content to LinkedIn™'s format and audience preferences. Use high-quality images and videos, as well as informative and engaging captions. Utilise LinkedIn™'s native features like polls, documents, and live videos to increase engagement.

5. Consistency and Frequency

Establish a consistent posting schedule to keep your audience engaged and build brand awareness. Whether it's daily event tips, weekly showcases, or monthly industry insights, maintain regular and consistent content to stay top-of-mind with your audience.

6. Measure and Iterate

Monitor the performance of your content regularly to understand what resonates with your audience. Track metrics such as engagement, reach, and conversion to evaluate the effectiveness of your content strategy. Use insights from your analytics to refine your approach and optimise future content for better results.

By implementing a robust content strategy on LinkedIn™, you can effectively showcase your expertise, build meaningful relationships with potential clients, and ultimately win more business. Just like a successful disco party, your content should be vibrant, engaging, and unforgettable.

CHOICE POINTS

If you want to learn more about strategy, turn to page 169.
To explore more about thought leadership, turn to page 182.
For analytics, go to page 10.

15. CURATED CONTENT

Just as a skilled DJ mixes both popular tracks and their own original mixes to keep the dance floor buzzing, business owners on LinkedIn™ should leverage both curated and created content to maintain an engaging and credible presence. Let's explore how these content types compare and why using both is crucial for establishing thought leadership.

What is Curated Content?
Curated content involves sharing valuable information from other sources within your industry; it's like a DJ playing well-known hits that resonate with the crowd.

Advantages:
- Saves time and resources
- Demonstrates industry awareness
- Provides diverse perspectives
- Builds relationships with other thought leaders

Disadvantages:
- Less control over the message
- Doesn't directly showcase your unique insights

Created Content

Created content is original material you produce yourself; it's akin to a DJ creating their own tracks or remixes.

Advantages:
- Showcases your unique expertise
- Builds your brand voice
- Provides complete control over the message
- Establishes you as a primary source of information

Disadvantages:
- More time-consuming to produce
- Requires consistent creativity and effort

C

CURATED CONTENT

Why Business Owners Should Use a Mix of Both Curated and Created Content

1. Establishes Credibility as a Thought Leader: By sharing a mix of curated and created content, you demonstrate both your industry knowledge and your unique insights. This balanced approach is like a DJ who knows all the popular tracks but also surprises the crowd with original mixes, establishing themselves as a true music connoisseur.

2. Becomes the Main Source of Information: When you consistently share valuable content, your LinkedIn™ profile becomes a go-to resource in your field. This is similar to how a renowned DJ's setlists become highly anticipated events.

3. Builds a Well-Rounded Presence: Curated content shows you're connected to industry trends, while created content showcases your expertise. This combination creates a well-rounded professional image, much like a versatile DJ who can cater to various musical tastes.

4. Enhances Engagement: Variety in content keeps your audience engaged. Just as a diverse playlist keeps party-goers on the dance floor, a mix of content types maintains interest in your LinkedIn™ presence.

5. Demonstrates Generosity: Sharing others' content (with proper attribution) shows you're not just self-promoting but genuinely interested in providing value to your network. This generosity can lead to reciprocal sharing and expanded reach.

Finding the Best Curated Sources

Industry Publications: Follow reputable journals and magazines in your field. These are like the top charts for a DJ, providing reliable, current information.

Thought Leaders: Identify and follow key influencers in your industry. Their insights can be valuable additions to your content mix, similar to how a DJ might feature guest artists. Turn on the notification bell so you don't miss any updates.

LinkedIn™ Groups: Join relevant professional groups to discover content shared by peers and experts. This is akin to attending industry showcases to discover new tracks.

C

CURATED CONTENT

<u>Content Curation Tools:</u> Find tools that can aggregate content from various sources. These tools act like a DJ's record collection, helping you organise and select the best content to share.

<u>Set Up Google Alerts:</u> Create alerts for key industry terms to stay updated on the latest news and trends. This is like having scouts who inform you about the hottest new tracks.

<u>Engage with Your Network:</u> Pay attention to what your connections are sharing. Sometimes the best content comes from your immediate professional circle, much like how local artists can provide fresh sounds to a DJ's repertoire.

A balanced approach using both curated and created content is key to establishing yourself as a thought leader on LinkedIn™. By sharing valuable insights from others alongside your own unique perspectives, you create a rich, engaging presence that positions you as a central figure in your industry. Just as a great DJ knows how to blend familiar hits with original tracks to keep the party going, a savvy business owner on LinkedIn™ uses a mix of content types to maintain an engaging and authoritative profile. Embrace this dual approach and watch your professional influence grow and your dance floor, or network, expand.

CHOICE POINTS

If you want to learn more about content strategy, turn to page 34.
To explore more about industry insights, turn to page 74.
To find out about bell notifications, go to page 19.

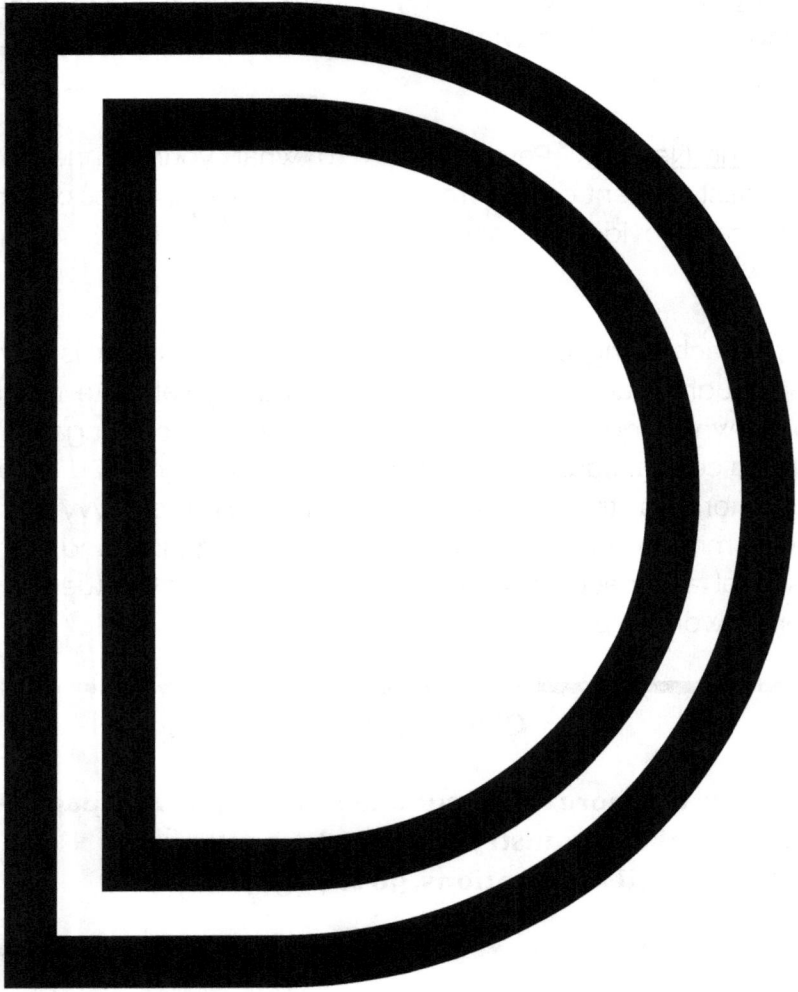

D

16. DATA INSIGHTS

At your party, you may like to keep a special guest book where you jot down all the information about your guests and their party preferences. This book helps you understand which party themes are most popular, who your most loyal guests are, and when is the best time to host certain types of events.

LinkedIn™ also has a 'special book', but instead of party preferences, it's filled with information about people's professional lives and interests. Businesses can use this information to understand their clients, connect with them, and grow their event-planning business. Here's how it works:

Understanding Your Clients
Just like your guest book helps you know which party themes to plan more of, LinkedIn™ data helps businesses understand their clients better. You can see things like where your clients work, what industries they're in, and what skills they have. This helps businesses tailor their event offerings and marketing messages to better meet their clients' needs.

Connecting with Clients
LinkedIn™ data also helps businesses connect with potential clients who might be interested in their events. By looking at things like job titles, company sizes, and locations, businesses can find people who are likely to enjoy their events and reach out to them with special offers or invitations to upcoming parties.

Growing the Business
Knowing your clients' favourite party themes helps you grow your business by planning more of what they love; LinkedIn™ data helps businesses grow by finding new clients and expanding their reach. By analysing data on trends and market demand, businesses can make informed decisions about where to host new events, which themes to introduce, and how to attract more clients.

Building Relationships
Finally, just like how getting to know your clients personally helps you build stronger relationships with them, businesses can use LinkedIn™ data to personalise their interactions with clients. By remembering details like people's job titles, interests, and past interactions, businesses can show clients that they care about them as individuals and value their patronage.

D

DATA INSIGHTS

When it comes to leveraging data insights on LinkedIn™, the most important thing is to focus on engagement metrics. Just as a great DJ pays attention to which songs get people on the dance floor, you should closely monitor which of your posts and content generate the most likes, comments, and shares.

Engagement metrics are the pulse of your LinkedIn™ presence, indicating what resonates with your audience. By understanding which topics, formats, and posting times drive the most interaction, you can refine your content strategy to keep your professional party buzzing with activity.

By leveraging LinkedIn™'s data, you can better understand its audience, connect with potential clients, grow the business strategically, and build lasting relationships. This data-driven approach ensures that every event is a hit, just like a perfectly planned party that everyone talks about for weeks.

CHOICE POINTS

If you want to learn more about analytics, turn to page 10.
To explore more about social listening, turn to page 163.
If you wish to delve deeper into industry insights, go to page 74.

DID YOU KNOW?

As of May 2024, a LinkedIn® benchmarks report found that the average engagement rate was 3.85%.

D

17. DIRECT MESSAGING

You may have a special party hotline that allows you to talk directly to your guests, no matter where they are. This is just like LinkedIn™ Direct Messaging, where you can chat with people one-on-one or in groups Here's how it works:

Sending Messages
Just like you can pick up the party hotline to call a guest and chat about their favourite party themes, on LinkedIn™, you can send messages to people you're connected with; it's a way to have private conversations with them.

Starting a Conversation
When you send a message it's like inviting someone to have a chat with you at your office. You might ask them about their favourite party ideas, share planning tips, or even discuss collaborating on a special event together.

Building Relationships
Just as talking to guests on the party hotline helps you get to know them better and build stronger relationships, messaging on LinkedIn™ allows you to connect with people in your professional network. You can learn more about their interests, share ideas, and explore potential business opportunities.

Keeping in Touch
The party hotline isn't just for one-time conversations – you can message guests anytime to check in, share updates, or discuss new event themes. Similarly, on LinkedIn™, you can continue conversations over time, keeping in touch with your connections and nurturing your relationships.

Using LinkedIn™ Direct Messaging effectively can enhance your networking efforts, foster collaboration, and strengthen your connections within the event-planning community. Just like a friendly chat over the party hotline can lead to unforgettable events, meaningful conversations on LinkedIn™ can open doors to new opportunities.

CHOICE POINTS

If you want to learn more about connection notes, turn to page 30.
To explore more about notifications, turn to page 110.

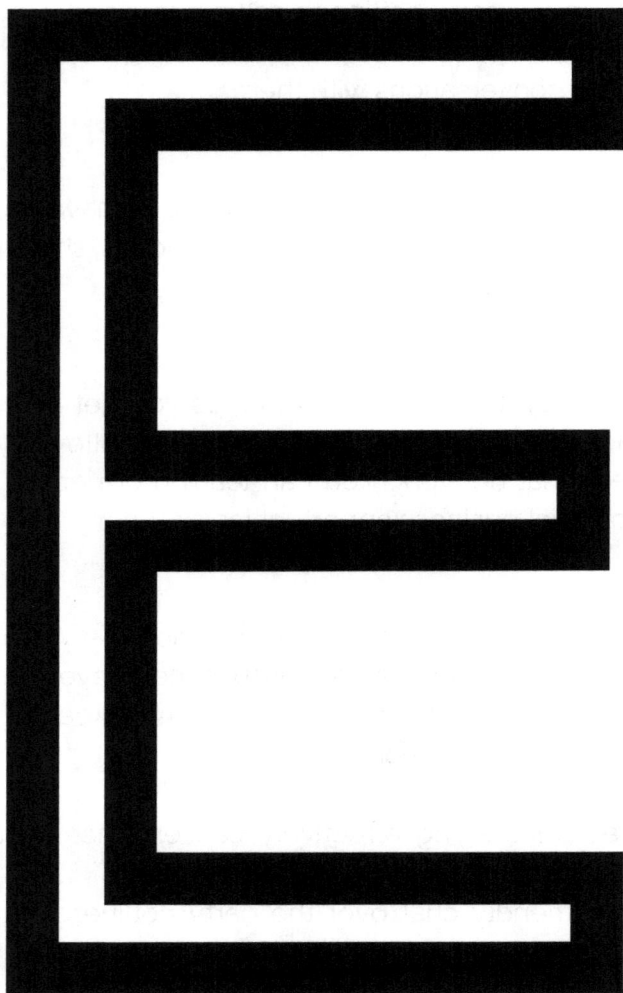

E

18. EMPLOYEE ADVOCACY

You may have a team of ambassadors, they love your events and want to tell everyone about them; they wear shirts with your company logo and spread the word about your business wherever they go.

LinkedIn™ Employee Advocacy works the same way. It's like having a team of party ambassadors who work at Party Perfection and use their LinkedIn™ profiles to talk about how amazing your events business is. Here's how it works:

Sharing Party Love
Just like your party ambassadors love sharing stories about your exciting events with guests who attend, employees can share stories about the business with their LinkedIn™ connections. They might post about new event themes, special promotions, or behind-the-scenes glimpses of the planning process.

Reaching More People
When your party ambassadors talk about your business on LinkedIn™, it's like spreading the word to a wider audience. Their LinkedIn™ connections might see their posts and become curious about your events, leading to more people discovering your exceptional party-planning services.

Building Trust
Your party ambassadors are like trusted friends recommending your events to others. When employees share positive experiences and testimonials about your business on LinkedIn™, it helps build trust and credibility with their connections. People are more likely to trust recommendations from people they know and respect.

Growing Your Business
By harnessing the power of Employee Advocacy on LinkedIn™, you can attract more clients, increase brand awareness, and ultimately grow your business. When employees become advocates for you on LinkedIn™, they become valuable partners in helping you achieve your business goals.

Employee Advocacy stats are accessed by an Admin of your Company Page. Here's how to make the most of employee advocacy stats on LinkedIn™:

EMPLOYEE ADVOCACY

E

Monitor Engagement Metrics:
Keep a close eye on likes, comments, and shares generated by employee-shared content.

These metrics are like measuring the buzz your team creates at the networking event. High engagement rates indicate that your employees' networks find the content valuable and relevant.

Track Reach and Impressions:
Analyse how far your employees' posts are travelling. This is similar to seeing how many new faces your team introduces to your brand at the party. A wider reach means your message is spreading to previously untapped audiences.

Measure Click-through Rates (CTR):
Monitor how many people are clicking on links shared by employees. This is like counting how many party-goers actually follow up on the conversations they've had with your team. A high CTR suggests that the content is compelling and relevant to the audience.

Analyse Audience Growth:
Keep tabs on the growth of your employees' professional networks. This is like tracking how many new connections your team makes at each networking event. A growing network means more potential eyes on your brand message.

Compare Employee vs. Corporate Account Performance:
Contrast the performance of content shared by employees with that shared on your official company page. Often, employee-shared content performs better, much like how personal introductions at a party can be more effective than formal company presentations.

By effectively utilising these employee advocacy statistics, companies can transform their LinkedIn™ presence from a solo performance to a full band, with each employee playing a crucial role in amplifying the brand's message and reach.

CHOICE POINTS

To learn more about company pages, turn to page 26.
To explore more about data insights, turn to page 40.
To find out about influencers, go to page 77.

E

19. ENDORSEMENTS

Imagine you have a special board where clients can leave little notes saying how much they love your events. These notes are endorsements; they're a way for people to publicly show their support for your business and recommend it to others. Here's how it works:

Showing Support
Just like leaving a note on your event board, endorsing someone on LinkedIn™ is a way to show support for their skills and abilities. It's like saying, "Hey, I've attended their party, and it was epic!"

Highlighting Skills
When someone endorses you on LinkedIn™, they're affirming that they believe you're really good at something, like planning unforgettable parties. It's a way for them to highlight your skills and talents to others in your professional network.

Building Reputation
The more endorsements you have on LinkedIn™, the more it shows that people trust and respect your abilities. It's like having lots of positive notes on your event board, it helps build your reputation and credibility.

Networking Opportunity
Endorsements can also help you connect with other event enthusiasts on LinkedIn™. When someone sees that you're endorsed for a particular skill, they might be more likely to reach out to you for advice, collaboration, or other opportunities.

By encouraging your clients and connections to endorse your skills on LinkedIn™, you can enhance your reputation, expand your network, and attract new clients. Just like those glowing notes on your board, endorsements serve as powerful testimonials that showcase the quality and impact of your business.

CHOICE POINTS

If you want to learn more about recommendations, turn to page 141.
To explore more about kudos, turn to page 85.
To find out more about testimonials, go to page 175.

E

20. ENGAGEMENT

Engagement on LinkedIn™ is like the energy on the dance floor at a disco party. It's not just about having a crowd; it's about how lively and interactive that crowd is. When people are actively participating, dancing, and having fun, the atmosphere becomes electric, just as engagement transforms your LinkedIn™ presence into a vibrant hub of activity.

Creating a Buzz: Just as a DJ reads the room to play tracks that get people moving, engagement on LinkedIn™ involves sharing content that resonates with your audience. When you post updates, articles, or insights that spark conversations, you create a buzz that draws people in, encouraging them to join the discussion.

Building Connections: Engagement is about more than just likes; it's about fostering relationships. Imagine a disco where party-goers are not only dancing but also mingling and chatting. On LinkedIn™, meaningful interactions, comments, shares, and discussions help you build connections with others in your industry, making your network feel more like a community.

Encouraging Participation: A lively dance floor thrives on participation. Similarly, when you engage with your audience by asking questions or encouraging feedback, you invite them to join the conversation. This interaction is like a call to the dance floor, prompting others to join in and share their thoughts.

Recognising Contributions: Just as a DJ might spotlight a dancer who's particularly impressive, acknowledging and responding to your audience's contributions fosters a sense of belonging. When you appreciate comments and engage with your followers, it encourages them to continue participating, creating a more dynamic environment.

Measuring Success: Engagement metrics are like the applause and cheers from the crowd. They tell you how well your content is resonating and whether your audience is enjoying the show. Monitoring likes, comments, shares, and overall interaction helps you refine your strategy, ensuring that your LinkedIn™ presence remains lively and relevant.

Creating Memorable Experiences: Ultimately, engagement is about creating memorable experiences for your audience. Just as a great disco leaves guests with lasting memories, engaging content and interactions on LinkedIn™ can establish your brand as a trusted source of information and connection.

ENGAGEMENT

E

Key Engagement Metrics to Track

Impressions:

This metric shows how many times your content has been displayed to users; it's like counting how many people have seen the dazzling lights of your disco ball. Higher impressions indicate that your content is reaching a wider audience.

Reactions:

Reactions include likes, celebrates, supports, loves, insightful, and curious responses to your posts. This is akin to the crowd cheering and dancing in response to your music, showing that your content is hitting the right notes.

Comments:

The number of comments on your posts reflects how well you're engaging your audience. Just as conversations spark on the dance floor, comments indicate that your content is encouraging discussion and interaction.

Shares:

Shares represent how many times your content has been shared by others. This is like party-goers spreading the word about your fantastic disco, helping to amplify your reach and visibility.

Engagement Rate:

Engagement rate is calculated by dividing the total number of interactions your content receives by the total number of impressions, and then multiplying by 100%.

By focusing on creating engaging content and fostering meaningful interactions, you can turn your LinkedIn™ presence into a virtual showcase of your expertise and build a thriving professional community around your brand.

CHOICE POINTS

If you want to learn more about content strategy, turn to page 34.
To explore more about data insights, turn to page 40.
If you wish to delve deeper into competitor analysis, go to page 28.

E

21. EVENTS

Picture LinkedIn™ Events as the hottest disco party in town, where professionals from all walks of life come together to groove to the beat of knowledge sharing and networking. Just like hosting an unforgettable disco night, LinkedIn™ Events offer businesses a fantastic opportunity to shine in the spotlight and connect with their audience in a dynamic, engaging way. Here's how LinkedIn™ Events can make your business the talk of the professional town:

Free Admission to the Party
LinkedIn™ Events are free to create, like throwing a party without worrying about venue costs. This means businesses of all sizes can host events, from small startups to large corporations, without breaking the bank.

Expand Your Guest List
Just as a great disco attracts people from all over, LinkedIn™ Events allow you to reach beyond your existing network. It's like having your party promoted across the city, drawing in new faces and potential connections.

VIP List at Your Fingertips
With LinkedIn™ Events, you can see who's RSVP'd, much like having a guest list at the door. This feature lets you know who's coming to your party, allowing you to prepare and tailor your content to your audience.

Dress Up Your Event Page
Customise your event page with eye-catching details, just as you'd decorate your disco with glittering lights and mirror balls. Add a compelling description, engaging visuals, and all the essential information to make your event irresistible.

After-Party Engagement
Even after the event, the conversation can continue. It's like having an after-party where guests can discuss their favourite moments. Use this opportunity to follow up with attendees and continue building relationships.

Measure Your Party's Success
LinkedIn™ provides analytics for your events, letting you see how your party performed. It's like counting how many people hit the dance floor and which songs got them moving the most.

E

EVENTS

Advantages of Using LinkedIn® Events:

1. Boosting Brand Visibility
Hosting events puts your brand in the spotlight, like being the host of the most talked-about party in town. It increases your visibility and positions you as a thought leader in your industry.

2. Lead Generation
Events are a great way to attract potential clients or partners; it's like having a guestbook at your party where people leave their contact details, excited to hear from you again.

3. Building Community
Regular events help build a community around your brand; it's like creating a group of disco enthusiasts who always look forward to your parties and spread the word.

4. Showcasing Expertise
Use events to demonstrate your knowledge and skills; it's akin to showing off your best dance moves, impressing the crowd with your expertise.

5. Networking Opportunities
Events facilitate connections between attendees; it's like introducing your friends to each other at your party, fostering new relationships and collaborations.

By leveraging LinkedIn™ Events, businesses can create their own professional disco, where ideas are shared, connections are made, and opportunities dance into view. So, put on your best business attire, cue the music of innovation, and let your LinkedIn™ Event be the professional party everyone's talking about.

CHOICE POINTS

If you want to learn more about building a brand, turn to page 21.
To explore more about target audience, turn to page 172.
To find out about lead Generation turn to page 89.

22. EXPERIENCE SECTION

E

Imagine your disco party has a special wall showcasing your greatest hits and performances. The Experience section on LinkedIn™ is just like that wall; it's where you display your professional journey and career highlights.

The Experience section is crucial because it's like your professional playlist, showcasing your career progression and key achievements. It helps visitors understand your background and expertise, much like how your top tracks define your style as a DJ.

How Does It Work?

The Experience section allows you to list your work history, including job titles, companies, dates of employment, and descriptions of your roles. It's designed to give a chronological overview of your career, like a timeline of your best performances.

What Should Be Included and Why?

To make your Experience section shine, consider including:

Current and Relevant Positions: Focus on roles that align with your current career goals. It's like featuring your latest hits rather than old tracks you no longer perform.

Key Achievements: Highlight your major accomplishments in each role. These are your platinum records—the standout moments that define your career.

Skills Utilised: Mention the key skills you used in each position. This helps the LinkedIn™ algorithm understand your expertise, like tagging your music with the right genres.

Quantifiable Results: Where possible, include metrics that demonstrate your impact; it's like sharing your chart rankings or audience numbers to prove your success.

Keywords: Use industry-relevant keywords to improve your searchability. This is similar to using popular song titles or artist names to attract more listeners.

Important Note: LinkedIn™ doesn't need to be an exact CV. Focus on including experiences that are current and relevant to what you're doing now. This helps the algorithm show your profile for your current expertise, rather than for skills or roles you've moved on from; it's like updating your setlist to feature your latest tracks, ensuring your audience knows what kind of performance to expect from you today.

E

EXPERIENCE SECTION

The Experience section on LinkedIn™ is your professional highlight reel, showcasing your career journey and key achievements. By focusing on current and relevant positions, highlighting major accomplishments, and using industry-specific keywords, you can create a compelling narrative that resonates with your target audience. Remember, it's about presenting your best and most current self, just like a DJ who keeps their playlist fresh and exciting for today's audience. So, get ready to showcase your professional greatest hits and let your LinkedIn™ profile be the chart-topper of your industry.

CHOICE POINTS

If you want to learn more about personal profile, turn to page 121.
To explore more about optimisation, turn to page 117.
For further insights on keywords, go to page 83.

TOP TIP

Include quantifiable achievements in your Experience section. Use numbers, percentages, and specific outcomes to demonstrate your impact. For example, 'Increased sales by 30% in six months' is much more compelling than simply stating 'Responsible for sales.'

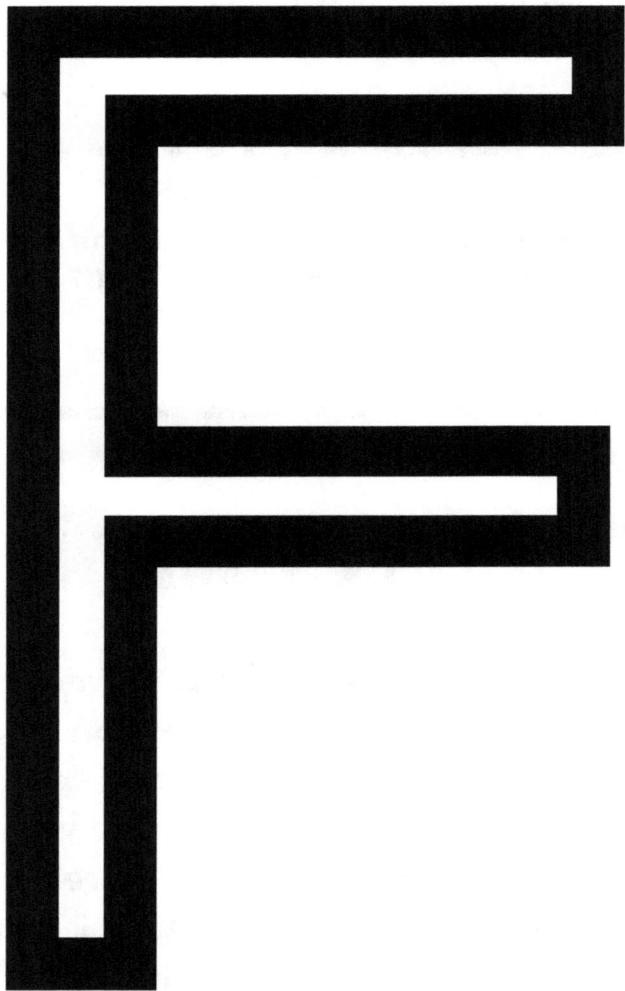

F

23. FEATURED SECTION

Imagine you're the coolest party planner in town, and you've just thrown the most amazing disco ever. You've got photos of the glittering dance floor, videos of people doing the funky chicken, and even a write up in the local paper about how brilliant it was. Now, wouldn't you want to show all of that off?

That's exactly what the Featured section on LinkedIn™ is all about. It's like your very own party highlight reel. Here's how it works:

Showcase Your Best Bits

The Featured section lets you display your top achievements and content; it's like creating a special display at the entrance of your disco, showing off photos of your best parties, your most popular playlists, and your shiniest disco ball.

On LinkedIn™, you can add posts, articles, links, and media to your Featured section to show visitors to your profile what you're most proud of.

Keep It Fresh

You can update your Featured section anytime.

Just like you'd change the decorations for each new party theme, you can switch up what's in your Featured section; this keeps your profile exciting and gives people a reason to come back and see what's new.

Advantages

1. Grab Attention

The Featured section is one of the first things people see on your profile; it's like having a massive, sparkly 'Welcome to the Party' sign that no one can miss!

2. Show, Don't Just Tell

You can demonstrate your skills and achievements visually. Instead of just saying you throw great parties, you're showing people the packed dance floor and happy faces.

The Featured section on LinkedIn™ is your chance to showcase your best work, keep your profile fresh, and grab people's attention right away.

Call to Action or Further Implication: So, put on your party-planner hat and think about what you'd want people to see first when they visit your profile; what will make them want to join your professional party?

F

FEATURED SECTION

Just like every great party needs the right mix of music, food, and decorations, your Featured section needs the right mix of content to make your profile shine. So, get creative and let your professional party begin.

CHOICE POINTS

If you want to learn more about optimisation, turn to page 117.
To explore more about keywords, turn to page 83.
To find out more about your personal profile, go to page 121.

TOP TIPS

In your Featured section include links to your online booking for easy scheduling, your digital products, or any other services you offer.
Position your most important offers at the top so they are the first thing visitors see.
By optimising the Featured section, you make it easier for potential clients or collaborators to connect with you, increasing your chances of converting visitors into leads.

F

24. FINDING LEADS

So, you're planning the biggest, most exciting party ever, and you want to invite all the coolest people who love to dance, enjoy great music, and have a fantastic time. But how do you find these partygoers and make sure they know about your event?

That's where finding leads on LinkedIn™ comes in; it's like discovering the perfect guests for your party, making sure they get an invite, and ensuring they're excited to join the fun. Here's how it works:

Identifying Potential Guests
Finding leads on LinkedIn™ starts with identifying potential clients or customers; it's like making a guest list for your party. You think about who would enjoy the music, the decorations, and the overall vibe. On LinkedIn™, you look for people who might be interested in your business by checking their job titles, industries, and interests.

Sending Invitations
Once you've identified potential leads, you can reach out to them. This is like sending out your party invitations. You want to make sure they know about your event and feel welcome to join. On LinkedIn™, you can send connection requests or InMail messages to introduce yourself and your business.

Engaging with Your Guests
After inviting potential leads, it's important to engage with them. At your party, you'd greet your guests, chat with them, and make sure they're having a good time. On LinkedIn™, you can engage by liking, commenting on, and sharing their posts, or by starting conversations in groups.

Creating Top-of-Mind Awareness
Regularly engaging with your leads' posts through notifications helps build top-of-mind awareness. When you consistently interact with their content, they are more likely to remember you when the time comes for them to make a decision; it's like the way a catchy tune or ear worm can linger in your head long after the music has stopped - your presence becomes memorable. Use the Bell Notification to ensure you don't miss anything.

F

FINDING LEADS

Following Up

Following up with leads ensures they stay interested. After the party, you might send thank you notes or share photos from the event to keep the excitement going. On LinkedIn™, follow up with messages or updates to keep the conversation going and build a relationship. Maybe ask them to subscribe to your newsletter.

Advantages

1. Increased Visibility

Finding leads on LinkedIn™ increases your business's visibility. It's like having more people know about your party, making it the talk of the town.

2. Targeted Audience

You can target specific audiences who are likely to be interested in your business. Just like inviting people who love the same kind of music and party atmosphere, you're reaching out to those who are most likely to enjoy and benefit from your services.

3. Building Relationships

Engaging with leads helps build strong professional relationships; it's like making new friends at your party who will remember the great time they had and look forward to your next event.

Finding leads on LinkedIn™ is like planning the perfect party - you identify potential guests, send out invitations, engage with them, and follow up to keep the excitement alive. Get ready to throw the best professional party ever by finding and engaging with your leads on LinkedIn™. Make sure they know about your business and are excited to be part of your network.

By using LinkedIn™ effectively, you can discover the perfect leads, build meaningful relationships, and grow your business, just like planning and hosting an unforgettable party.

CHOICE POINTS

If you want to learn more about building a brand, turn to page 21.
To explore more about bell notifications, go to page 19
To find out about your service page, go to page 156.

F

25.FOLLOWERS

You're throwing an incredible disco party, complete with flashing lights, a glittering disco ball, and the best music in town. Some people are on the dance floor, fully involved in the fun, while others are standing at the edges, watching and enjoying the atmosphere without joining in. These watchers are like followers on LinkedIn™. Here's how it works:

Understanding Followers
Followers on LinkedIn™ are people who want to keep up with your updates but aren't directly connected to you; it's like having guests at your party who enjoy the vibe but aren't dancing yet. They're interested in what you're doing and want to see what you share.

Receiving Updates
Just as your party guests can see the fun happening on the dance floor, followers can see your posts, articles, and updates on LinkedIn™. They're watching from the sidelines, eager to see what you create and share, even if they haven't joined your inner circle yet.

Engaging with Content
Followers can interact with your content by liking, commenting, or sharing your posts; it's like when someone at your party starts clapping along to the music or chatting with others about how great the event is. Their engagement shows they appreciate what you're doing, even if they're not fully participating.

Building Your Audience
Having followers helps you grow your audience. Just like the more people who see your party and talk about it, the more likely it is that others will want to join in next time. On LinkedIn™, followers can help spread the word about your expertise and attract new connections to your profile.

Advantages
1. Increased Reach
Followers expand your reach on LinkedIn™; it's like having a crowd at your party who can tell their friends how fantastic it was, leading to even more people wanting to join in the future.

2. Building Credibility
The more followers you have, the more credible you appear. Just as a packed dance floor shows that your party is a hit, having many followers indicates that people value your insights and expertise.

57

F

FOLLOWERS

3. Opportunities for Engagement

Followers can become potential connections or clients; it's like those party guests who, after watching the fun, decide they want to join in and dance. Engaging with your followers can turn them into active participants in your professional network.

Having followers on LinkedIn™ is like having an audience at your disco party. They enjoy your content, cheer you on, and can help spread the word about your amazing business. By nurturing these relationships, you can turn followers into connections and create a vibrant network that supports your business goals. So, keep sharing your best party-planning tips and insights, and watch your follower count grow.

CHOICE POINTS

If you want to learn more about connections, turn to page 34.
To explore more about target audience, turn to page 177.
To find out more about engagement, turn to page 57.

DID YOU KNOW?

In November 23, Social Insider found that for accounts with over 100,000 followers, the median likes are highest for multiple image posts (150 likes).

26. GROUPS

Think about your disco party where everyone is dancing, chatting, and having a great time. Now imagine there's a special VIP area where people who love the same music can gather, share their thoughts, and connect with each other. This is similar to what LinkedIn™ groups offer, a place for professionals with shared interests to come together. Here's how it works:

Joining the Right Crowd
Being part of a LinkedIn™ group allows you to connect with people who share your interests or work in your industry; it's like joining a special dance circle at your party where everyone loves the same tunes. You can learn from each other, share ideas, and support one another.

Sharing Ideas and Insights
In a LinkedIn™ group, you can share your expertise, ask questions, and contribute to discussions. This is like having a group of friends at your party who are all excited to talk about their favourite songs and dance moves. Sharing your knowledge helps you stand out and shows others what you bring to the table.

Networking Opportunities
Being active in groups can open up networking opportunities. Just as you might meet new friends at your party who could become your next dance partners, connecting with members in a LinkedIn™ group can lead to valuable professional relationships. You never know who might need your services or have a great opportunity for you!

Staying Updated on Trends
LinkedIn™ groups often discuss the latest trends and news in your industry. It's like hearing the newest hits at your party that everyone is buzzing about. Staying informed helps you keep your skills sharp and ensures you're always in the loop.

Advantages

1. Enhanced Visibility
Participating in LinkedIn™ groups increases your visibility among peers and potential clients; it's like being the star of the dance floor, where everyone can see your moves and wants to join in on the fun.

GROUPS

2. Building Authority

By sharing your insights and engaging in discussions, you establish yourself as an authority in your field. Just as a great DJ knows how to keep the party going, being knowledgeable in your group makes others look to you for advice and guidance.

3. Access to Resources

Groups often share valuable resources, tips, and tools that can help you in your professional journey; it's like having a group of friends at your party who share their best dance tips and tricks, making everyone better dancers.

Being part of LinkedIn™ groups is like having a special area at your disco party where you can connect, share, and learn from others who love the same things you do. By joining and actively participating in these groups, you can enhance your professional network, build your reputation, and stay updated on industry trends. So, find the right groups, jump in, and start dancing your way to success on LinkedIn™.

CHOICE POINTS

If you want to learn more about thought leadership, turn to page 182.
To explore more about networking, turn to page 101.
To find out about social listening, go to page 163.

DID YOU KNOW?

There are more than 2 million LinkedIn® Groups and according to Kinsta over 8 million professionals are part of industry-specific LinkedIn® Groups.

27. GUIDELINES

Picture a disco party where everyone's having a fantastic time, but there are some basic rules to ensure everyone stays safe and has fun. LinkedIn™ has its own set of guidelines, like the rules at your party, to keep things professional and enjoyable for all users. Here's how they work:

Be Professional
LinkedIn™ is all about professional networking; it's like wearing your best disco outfit to the party - you want to look your best and make a good impression. Keep your posts, comments, and interactions professional and work-related.

Respect Others
Just as you'd treat other partygoers with respect, do the same on LinkedIn™. Be kind in your interactions, avoid offensive language, and respect others' opinions; it's like making sure everyone feels welcome on the dance floor.

Share Authentic Content
Post genuine, original content; it's like bringing your own unique dance moves to the party instead of copying someone else's. Avoid plagiarism and always give credit where it's due if you are sharing or curating content.

Protect Privacy
Be mindful of privacy, both yours and others; it's like not sharing embarrassing photos from the party without permission. Don't share personal information or confidential business details on LinkedIn™.

No Spam or Self-Promotion
Avoid excessive self-promotion or spamming; it's like not hogging the microphone at the karaoke corner of your party. Share valuable content and engage in meaningful conversations instead.

Use Appropriate Imagery
Choose professional profile pictures and cover images. Think of it as dressing appropriately for a work party rather than a beach bash. Your images should represent you in a professional light. Ensure you use pictures for which you have copyright permission.

GUIDELINES

Engage Thoughtfully

Participate in discussions and comment on posts in a constructive manner; it's like joining conversations at your party that add value and keep the good vibes flowing.

Advantages of Following Guidelines

1. Building a Positive Reputation

Following LinkedIn™'s guidelines helps you build a positive professional reputation; it's like being known as the person who throws the best, most respectful parties in town.

2. Creating a Safe Environment

When everyone follows the rules, it creates a safe and comfortable environment for all users; it's like ensuring everyone at your party feels secure and can enjoy themselves without worry.

3. Maximising Networking Opportunities

By adhering to guidelines, you increase your chances of making meaningful connections; it's like being the friendly, respectful person at the party that everyone wants to dance and chat with.

Following LinkedIn™'s guidelines is like being a great host at your disco party. You want to create an environment where everyone feels welcome, respected, and can have a good time while networking professionally. By sticking to these rules, you'll make the most of your LinkedIn™ experience and keep the professional party going strong.

CHOICE POINTS

If you want to learn more about privacy settings, turn to page 131.
To explore more about reputation management, turn to page 146.
To find out about curated content, go to page 37.

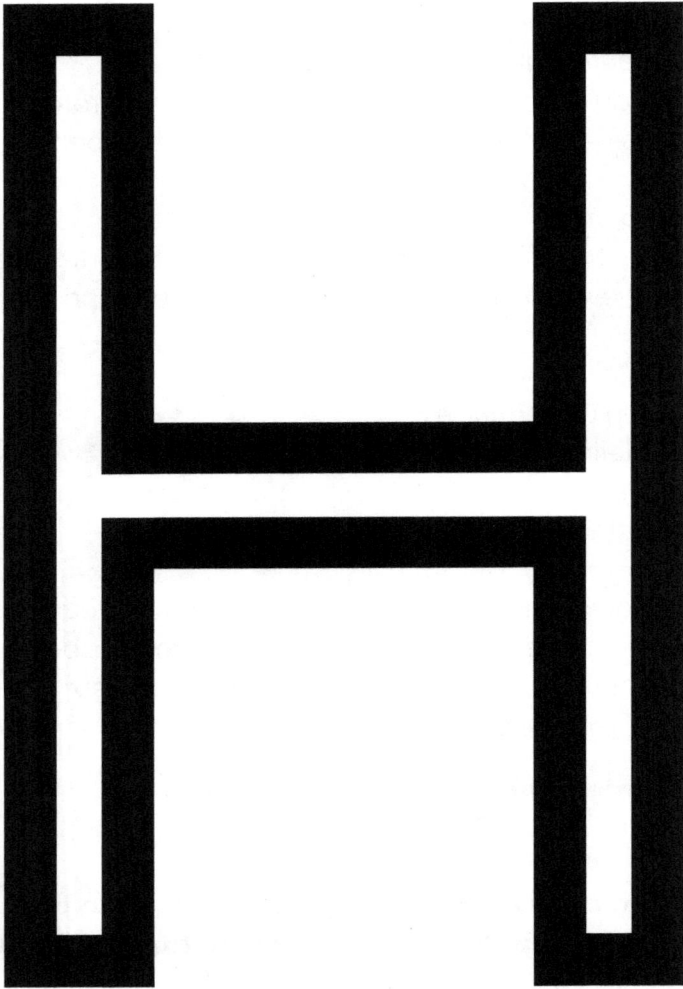

H

28. HASHTAGS
Are Hashtags Still Relevant on LinkedIn™?

Think of your disco party, where the music is pumping and the dance floor is alive with energy; you might use themed decorations to attract guests who love a particular vibe. Hashtags on LinkedIn™ help draw attention to your posts and connect you with the right audience. So, are hashtags still relevant, or have keywords taken over? Let's explore:

Visibility and Discovery
Hashtags are like the flashing lights at your party, guiding people to the fun. When you include relevant hashtags in your LinkedIn™ posts, they can appear in the feeds of users who follow those hashtags, even if they don't follow you. This means more people can discover your content, just like the way a catchy song can pull more dancers onto the floor.

Networking and Engagement
Using hashtags effectively can enhance your networking opportunities; they allow you to connect with professionals who share your interests, similar to the way a themed area at your party brings together people who love the same music. Engaging with posts under specific hashtags can lead to meaningful interactions and new connections.

Keyword Integration
While keywords are essential for making your content searchable, hashtags complement them by categorising your posts. Think of hashtags as the party invitations that let people know what to expect; they help the LinkedIn™ algorithm understand your expertise and interests, creating a stronger presence for you online.

Best Practices for Using Hashtags

1.*Research Relevant Hashtags:* Before posting, check out which hashtags are popular in your industry. This is like choosing the right theme for your party to attract the right crowd.

2.*Limit the Number of Hashtags:* Using one to three hashtags per post is generally recommended. This keeps your content focused, just like not overcrowding the dance floor with too many people.

H

HASHTAGS

3.Capitalise Words in Hashtags: For better readability, use Pascal Case (capitalising the first letter of each word, this is also sometimes called Camel Case) in multiword hashtags. This makes it easier for everyone to understand your tags, just as clear signage helps guests find their way around the party.

4.Follow Hashtags: You can follow specific hashtags to stay updated on topics relevant to your interests and industry. This is like keeping an ear out for the latest hits at the party, ensuring you're in tune with current discussions and trends.

Hashtags are still very much relevant on LinkedIn™ and should be a key part of your content strategy. They enhance visibility, facilitate networking, and work hand-in-hand with keywords. By using hashtags thoughtfully, you can expand your reach and connect with a broader audience, making your presence on LinkedIn™ as vibrant and exciting as the best disco party in town.

CHOICE POINTS

If you want to learn more about visibility, turn to page 197.
To explore more about keywords, turn to page 83.
For further insights on tags and mentions, go to page 174.

TOP TIP

LinkedIn® features a dedicated 'Explore' tab where you can find trending hashtags related to current events and popular topics in your industry. This is a great starting point for identifying hashtags that are currently gaining traction.

H

29. HEADLINE

Your LinkedIn™ headline is like the dazzling neon sign outside your disco party; it's the first thing people see, and it needs to grab their attention and make them want to step inside. This is the most important aspect of your profile. First impressions count.

Why is it Important?

Your LinkedIn™ headline is crucial because it gives others a snapshot of who you are and what you do; it's like the catchy title of your party that tells everyone what kind of fun they can expect. A strong headline can attract potential clients and connections, making it essential for building your professional brand.

Character Limit and Importance

Your LinkedIn™ headline can be up to 220 characters long, but the first 60 characters are the most important. These 60 characters are like the bold letters on your party invitation, they're what people see first and remember most. Aim for 30-50 words in total to make the most of this space.

Search Engine Visibility

Your LinkedIn™ headline shows up in Google search results, making it a powerful tool for your online presence; it's like having your party advertised on the biggest billboard in town, everyone can see it.

Algorithm Impact

The headline is one of the most important fields for LinkedIn™'s search algorithm. It helps determine how often you appear in search results, just as the popularity of your party theme might determine how many people hear about it.

Industry Credibility

Your LinkedIn™ headline portrays you as a credible member of your industry; it's like being known as the go-to person for throwing the best themed parties in town.

Speaking Your Client's Language

Your LinkedIn™ headline is like your professional tagline; it's one of the first things people see when they find you online. By using words and phrases that your ideal clients use themselves, you make it easy for them to understand what you do; it's like describing your services in a way that immediately clicks with them, helping them quickly decide if you're the right person for their needs.

H

HEADLINE
Create a headline that works!

To create a headline that works hard for you, be succinct, creative, and include key terms that make it easy for others to understand what you do and why. Consider using this template:

[Your Job Title] | [Your Key Skills or Specialisation] | [Value Proposition or Unique Selling Point] | [Call to action]

Example:
Party Planner Extraordinaire | Event Coordination | Creating Unforgettable Experiences | DM me to chat

Tips for Crafting Your Headline

1.*Be Specific:* Just like specifying the theme of your disco (e.g., '80s Night), be clear about your role and expertise.

2. *Use Keywords:* Incorporate relevant keywords that potential connections might search for. This is like using popular song titles to attract more dancers.

3. *Show Personality:* Add a touch of your personality to make it memorable. Just as a fun emoji can spark curiosity, a unique headline can make you stand out.

Your LinkedIn™ headline is like the vibrant sign that invites people to your disco party; it should be eye-catching, informative, and reflective of your professional identity. By crafting a compelling headline, you're setting the stage for a great first impression and increasing your visibility in the professional world. Go, get ready to light up LinkedIn™ and make a lasting impression with your headline.

CHOICE POINTS

If you want to learn more about keywords, turn to page 83.
To explore more about your unique value proposition, turn to page 188.
To find out more about your ideal client, go to page 177.

H

30. HIRING

Imagine your disco party is in full swing, and you need to find the perfect people to help you create an unforgettable experience. Hiring on LinkedIn™ is like assembling a dream team of party planners, DJs, and decorators to ensure your event is a hit.

Why is Hiring on LinkedIn® Important?
Hiring on LinkedIn™ is essential because it connects you with a vast pool of talent. Just as you want the best DJs and entertainers to keep the energy high at your party, you want to find skilled professionals who can contribute to your business. LinkedIn™ allows you to tap into a network of over 1 billion members, making it easier to find the right fit for your team.

How to Use LinkedIn® for Hiring

Post Job Openings
Just like putting up flashy signs to announce your party, you can post job openings on your LinkedIn™ company page to attract potential candidates. Make sure your job descriptions are clear and engaging, highlighting what makes your company a great place to work.

Utilise the Open To Work Feature
This feature is like having a special VIP area at your party where job seekers can signal that they're ready to join the fun; you can easily find candidates who are actively looking for opportunities.

Search for Candidates
Use LinkedIn™'s powerful search tools to find individuals with the skills and experience you need; it's like scouting for the best dancers at your party, look for those who stand out.

Engage with Your Network
Just as you would mingle with guests at your party, engage with your LinkedIn™ connections. Ask for referrals or recommendations, as your network can help you find great candidates.

H

HIRING

Advantages of Hiring on LinkedIn®

1. *Wider Reach:* Posting jobs on LinkedIn™ allows you to reach a global audience; it's like sending out invitations to party-goers from all over the world, ensuring you have a diverse group of attendees.

2 *Access to Passive Candidates*: Many talented professionals may not be actively looking for jobs but are open to new opportunities. LinkedIn™ helps you connect with these passive candidates, just like discovering hidden gems at your party who are ready to shine.

3. *Showcase Your Company Culture:* Use your LinkedIn™ profile to showcase your company culture and values. This is like creating an inviting atmosphere at your party, making potential candidates excited to join your team.

Hiring on LinkedIn™ is like assembling the ultimate team for your disco party. By leveraging the platform's features, you can connect with a wide range of talented professionals, ensuring your business has the right people to succeed. So, get ready to light up your hiring process and find the perfect candidates to help your business thrive.

CHOICE POINTS

If you want to learn more about company pages, turn to page 26.
To explore more about employee advocacy, turn to page 43.
To find out more about industry insights, turn to page 74.

31. IMAGES

Your disco party is in full swing, with vibrant lights, energetic music, and guests dancing the night away. Now, imagine how much more exciting it would be if you had stunning visuals showcasing the fun and excitement of the event. Images on LinkedIn™ are just as important; they grab attention, convey messages, and enhance your professional presence.

Images are crucial on LinkedIn™ because they make your posts more engaging and visually appealing. Just like eye-catching decorations can draw people to your party, compelling images can attract viewers to your content. Posts with images receive significantly more engagement than those without, making them a powerful tool for capturing attention and encouraging interaction.

Creating a Strong First Impression
Your profile picture and cover image are often the first things people see when they visit your LinkedIn™ profile. These visuals serve as your first impression, much like the entrance to your party. A professional and inviting image can set the tone for how others perceive you and your brand.

Recommended Image Sizes
To ensure your images look their best on LinkedIn™, here are some recommended sizes:

Profile Picture: 400 x 400 pixels. This is your personal branding image, so make sure it's clear and professional, like a well-taken photo at your party.

Cover Banner: 1584 x 396 pixels. This is your chance to showcase your personality or business theme, similar to the vibrant decorations that create the atmosphere at your event.

Shared Images: 1200 x 627 pixels. When sharing posts or articles, use this size to ensure your images display correctly in feeds, just like making sure your party flyers are eye-catching and easy to read.

Images on LinkedIn™ are essential for making a strong impression and engaging your audience. By using the right sizes and ensuring your visuals are professional and appealing, you can enhance your profile and posts, drawing more people to your professional 'party'. Get creative with your images, showcase your brand, and let your LinkedIn™ presence shine as brightly as the lights at your disco.

IMAGES

CHOICE POINTS

If you want to learn more about your profile photo, turn to page 134.
To explore more about your banner, go to page 17.
To find out about videos, go to page 194.

DID YOU KNOW?

Research suggests that authentic, high-quality, and relevant images tend to perform better in terms of user engagement and conversion rates compared with generic stock photos.

32. INDUSTRY INSIGHTS

Industry insights offer valuable information and trends that provide a deeper understanding of the market landscape, consumer behaviour, and emerging developments within a particular sector. For business owners on LinkedIn™, sharing and engaging with industry insights is crucial for establishing credibility and positioning themselves as thought leaders. Just as a DJ doesn't simply play tracks but adds their unique flair and transitions to create an unforgettable party atmosphere, business owners should not only reshare information but also add their personal perspectives and thoughts. This approach enhances engagement and showcases your expertise, making your contributions more impactful.

The Importance of Industry Insights

Establishing Credibility

Sharing relevant industry insights helps business owners build credibility as thought leaders. By consistently providing valuable information and adding your unique perspective, you position yourself as a knowledgeable source in your field. This is much like a DJ who is respected for their deep understanding of music trends and genres. Just as a DJ curates their setlist based on the latest hits and timeless classics, business owners can curate insights that resonate with their audience while infusing their own commentary.

Becoming a Main Source of Information

When you regularly share insights and your thoughts on them, your LinkedIn™ profile can become a go-to resource for your network. This is similar to how a well-known DJ becomes the primary source of entertainment at a party, drawing in guests who want to experience their unique sound. By being the first to share critical insights and adding your analysis, you can enhance your visibility and attract more connections.

Engaging Your Audience

Industry insights can spark discussions and engagement among your connections. By sharing thought-provoking articles, reports, or trends and adding your perspective, you encourage dialogue and interaction. This is like a DJ energising the crowd with a captivating performance. Engaged audiences are more likely to share your content, further amplifying your reach.

INDUSTRY INSIGHTS

Staying Ahead of the Competition

Keeping up to date with industry trends allows business owners to anticipate changes and adapt their strategies accordingly. This proactive approach is like a DJ who stays updated on new music releases and emerging genres, ensuring their sets remain fresh and relevant. By adding your insights, you can also highlight how these trends impact your specific niche.

Industry insights are invaluable for business owners looking to establish themselves as thought leaders on LinkedIn™. By sharing relevant information and engaging with trends while adding your unique perspective, you can enhance your credibility, become a primary source of information, and foster meaningful connections within your network. Just as a skilled DJ curates their setlist to create an unforgettable experience, business owners can curate industry insights and infuse their thoughts to build a compelling professional presence. Embrace the power of industry insights, and watch your influence and opportunties grow.

Networking Opportunities

Sharing insights can attract like-minded professionals and potential collaborators. When you position yourself as an expert by not just sharing information but also providing your analysis, others are more likely to reach out for advice, partnerships, or opportunities, just as a DJ might collaborate with other artists to create new sounds and experiences.

How Business Owners Can Find the Best Industry Insights

1. *Follow Industry Leaders:* Connect with and follow influential figures in your industry. Their posts and articles often contain valuable insights and trends. This is like a DJ following other artists to discover new music and stay current.

2. *Subscribe to Industry Publications:* Regularly read trade journals, magazines, and online publications relevant to your field. These sources provide in-depth analyses and reports, similar to how a DJ studies music reviews and charts to curate their playlsts.

3. *Join Professional Groups:* Participate in LinkedIn™ groups related to your industry. These groups often share valuable insights and discussions that can enhance your understanding of current trends, much like networking with fellow DJs to exchange knowledge and experiences.

I

INDUSTRY INSIGHTS

4. Attend Webinars and Conferences: Engage in industry webinars and conferences to gain insights directly from experts. In the same way that a DJ would attend music festivals where they can learn from top DJs and discover new trends in the industry.

.5. Utilise Content Curation Tools: Use tools to aggregate content from various sources. These tools can help you stay organised and ensure you're sharing the most relevant insights, just as a DJ maintains a well-organised library of tracks to choose from.

6. Set Up Google Alerts: Create alerts for specific keywords related to your industry. This will keep you updated on the latest news and trends, similar to the way a DJ keeps an ear out for new releases that could enhance their sets.

7. Use the bell notification: Using the bell notification feature on LinkedIn™ is crucial for staying abreast of industry insights and trends. When you click the bell icon on a connection's profile, you ensure that you receive notifications every time they post new content. This is particularly important for keeping up with thought leaders, industry experts, and competitors who can provide valuable information and updates relevant to your field.

8. Follow trending topics: Following trending topics on LinkedIn™ is vital for staying updated with industry insights, much like keeping an ear to the ground at a lively party to catch the latest buzz. When you pay attention to what's trending, you're essentially tuning into the hottest conversations and themes that everyone is talking about. This allows you to stay informed about the latest developments, challenges, and innovations in your field.

CHOICE POINTS

If you want to learn more about trending topics, turn to page 184.
To explore more about curated content, turn to page 37.
If you wish to delve deeper into thought leadership, go to page 182.

I

33. INFLUENCERS

Your disco party is the talk of the town, and everyone wants to know who's behind the fantastic music, vibrant lights, and unforgettable atmosphere. Influencers on LinkedIn™ are like the popular DJs and party planners who have the power to attract a crowd and create buzz. They play a crucial role in shaping conversations and trends within their industries.

Influencers on LinkedIn™ are essential because they help amplify your message and increase your visibility. Just as a well known DJ can draw in a larger audience to your party, industry influencers can introduce your content to their followers, expanding your reach and credibility. Their endorsement can lead to new connections, opportunities, and a stronger professional presence.

Building Relationships with Influencers

Connecting with influencers is like inviting the coolest partygoers to your event. You want to engage with them by commenting on their posts, sharing their content, and participating in discussions. This interaction can help you build relationships and establish yourself within your industry, just as mingling with popular guests can elevate the vibe of your party.

How to Leverage Influencers on LinkedIn®

Follow Influencers
Start by following industry leaders and influencers relevant to your field. This is like keeping an eye on the hottest DJs to see what music they're playing. By following them, you can stay updated on their insights and trends.

Engage with Their Content
Actively comment on and share their posts. Just as you would cheer for a great performance at your party, showing appreciation for their content can help you get noticed. Thoughtful engagement can lead to meaningful interactions and potential collaborations.

Create Valuable Content
Share your own insights and expertise to position yourself as a thought leader. This is like showcasing your own dance moves at the party - when you shine, others take notice. Use relevant hashtags and tag influencers in your posts to increase visibility.

INFLUENCERS

Join Relevant Groups

Participate in LinkedIn™ groups where influencers are active. This is like finding a special corner at your party where the best conversations happen. Engaging in these groups can help you connect with influencers and other professionals in your industry.

Use the bell notification

Using the bell notification feature on LinkedIn™ is essential for staying in tune with influencers in your industry, much like having your ear to the speakers at a party to catch the latest hits. When you click the bell icon on an influencer's profile, you ensure that you receive notifications every time they drop new content. By regularly engaging with their posts, you not only gain access to important information but also position yourself as an informed participant in the conversation.

Advantages of Engaging with Influencers

1. Increased Visibility: Collaborating with or being mentioned by influencers can significantly boost your visibility. Just as a famous DJ can fill a dance floor, an influencer's endorsement can attract more eyes to your profile and content.

2. Credibility and Trust: Being associated with respected influencers enhances your credibility; it's like being seen dancing with the coolest crowd at your party - it shows that you're part of the ingroup.

3. Networking Opportunities: Engaging with influencers can open doors to new connections and opportunities. Just as meeting new friends at a party can lead to exciting collaborations, connecting with influencers can help you expand your professional network.

Influencers on LinkedIn™ are like the star performers at your disco party, helping to create excitement and draw in a crowd. By following, engaging with, and building relationships with these industry leaders, you can enhance your visibility, credibility, and networking opportunities. So, get ready to dance with the influencers on LinkedIn™ and let your professional presence shine.

CHOICE POINTS

To learn more about groups, turn to page 60.
To explore more about visibility, turn to page 197.
To explore thought leadership, go to page 182.

J

J

34. JARGON

At the party everyone's having a great time, dancing and mingling. Now imagine if the DJ started using complex music terms or industry jargon that most guests didn't understand; it would create confusion and disconnect, wouldn't it? The same principle applies to your LinkedIn™ presence.

Why Avoiding Jargon is Important

Using clear, simple language on LinkedIn™ is like choosing music that everyone at your party can enjoy and dance to; it ensures your message is understood by a wider audience, not just industry insiders. This approach is crucial for several reasons:

Wider Reach

By avoiding jargon, acronyms, and complex terms, you make your content accessible to a broader audience; it's like playing popular hits at your party that everyone knows and loves, rather than obscure tracks only a few appreciate.

Better Engagement

When people understand your message easily, they're more likely to engage with your content. This is similar to how guests are more likely to dance when they recognise the music.

Improved Search Visibility

Using the language and vocabulary your target audience uses can significantly improve your search visibility; it's like advertising your party with terms that potential guests would actually search for, making it easier for them to find you.

How to Communicate Clearly on LinkedIn®

Use Plain Language: Instead of industry-specific terms, opt for simpler alternatives that convey the same meaning. This is like explaining the party theme in a way that everyone can understand and get excited about.

Spell Out Acronyms: If you must use an acronym, spell it out the first time you use it. This is like introducing a new dance move at your party by demonstrating it first before giving it a catchy name.

J

JARGON

Consider Your Audience: Think about who you're trying to reach and use language they're familiar with; it's like choosing music that appeals to your specific party crowd.

Use Keywords Wisely: Incorporate keywords that your target audience is likely to search for. This is similar to using popular song titles or dance styles in your party invitations to attract the right crowd.

Advantages of Clear Communication

1. Increased Visibility

Using common terms and phrases can help your content appear in more search results, both on LinkedIn™ and search engines. This is like having your party show up in local event listings, making it easier for people to find.

2. Better Connections

Clear communication helps you connect with professionals from various backgrounds, not just those in your immediate field. This is like having a diverse group of guests at your party, creating a more vibrant and interesting atmosphere.

3. Enhanced Credibility

By explaining complex ideas in simple terms, you demonstrate your expertise and ability to communicate effectively. This is like being the party host who can make everyone feel welcome and included, regardless of their background.

Avoiding jargon on LinkedIn™ is like ensuring your disco party is welcoming and enjoyable for all guests. By using clear, accessible language and focusing on keywords your audience uses, you can increase your visibility, engage more effectively with your network, and build stronger professional relationships. So, turn down the complex beats and turn up the crowd-pleasers in your LinkedIn™ communications.

CHOICE POINTS

If you want to learn more about visibility, turn to page 197.

To explore more about your target audience, turn to page 177.

To find out more about content strategy, turn to page 34.

K

K

35. KEYWORDS

Think of keywords on LinkedIn™ as the catchy tunes and popular songs at your disco party; they're what attract people to the dance floor, making sure everyone knows what kind of music to expect and encouraging them to join in the fun. Keywords play a crucial role in ensuring your profile and content are easily discoverable by the right audience.

Keywords on LinkedIn™ are specific terms or phrases that describe your skills, experience, and industry. They help the LinkedIn™ algorithm understand what your profile and posts are about, much like how a playlist sets the mood for your party. These keywords are essential for appearing in search results and attracting the right connections.

Why Are Keywords Important?

Visibility: Keywords help your profile and posts appear in search results, making it easier for others to find you; it's like having your party listed in event guides so more people know about it.

Relevance: They ensure that your content reaches the right audience, just as playing the right music attracts the crowd you want at your party.

Engagement: Keywords can increase engagement by making your content more discoverable and relevant to those searching for specific terms.

Where Can Keywords Be Used?

Keywords can be strategically placed throughout your LinkedIn™ profile and posts to maximise their effectiveness:

1.*Profile Headline:* This is like the marquee sign outside your party, giving a quick snapshot of what's inside. Include key terms that describe your role and expertise.

2. *About Section:* Use keywords to detail your experience and skills, much like describing the highlights of your party to entice guests.

3.*Experience Section:* Incorporate relevant terms in job titles and descriptions to showcase your professional journey.

K

KEYWORDS

4. Skills and Endorsements: List your top skills using keywords to make it clear what you're good at, similar to listing the best features of your party.

5. Posts and Articles: Use keywords in your content to increase its visibility and reach, just like promoting your party with popular themes and hashtags.

How to Find the Right Keywords for Your Business

Finding the right keywords is like choosing the perfect playlist for your party. Here's how you can do it:

Research Industry Terms: Look at job descriptions, industry reports, and competitor profiles to identify common terms. This is like checking out what music other popular parties are playing.

Use LinkedIn® Search: Type potential keywords into the LinkedIn™ search bar to see how often they appear and what kind of content they bring up. This helps you understand what terms are trending.

Analyse Top Profiles: Look at the profiles of industry leaders and influencers to see what keywords they use; it's like seeing what songs the best DJs are spinning.

Leverage Tools: Use keyword research tools to find high traffic terms relevant to your field. These tools are like having a DJ's playlist to ensure you're playing the hits.

Keywords on LinkedIn™ are essential for making your profile and content discoverable, relevant, and engaging. By strategically using keywords in your profile and posts, you can attract the right audience, increase your visibility, and ensure your professional presence is as lively and inviting as the best disco party. So, tune into the right keywords, and watch your LinkedIn™ engagement soar.

CHOICE POINTS

If you want to learn more about optimisation, turn to page 117.
To explore more about research, turn to page 149.
To find out more about visibility, go to page 197.

K

36. KUDOS

Giving kudos on LinkedIn™ is a way to recognise and show appreciation for someone's contributions and achievements within your professional network. Just like giving a shoutout to a friend at your disco party for their awesome dance moves, kudos allow you to celebrate the efforts of colleagues and connections in a meaningful way.

LinkedIn™ Kudos are represented by colourful icons, each symbolising a different type of recognition. There are ten types of Kudos, including:

Thank You: For expressing gratitude.
Going Above and Beyond: For those who exceed expectations.
Inspirational Leader: For individuals who lead by example.
Team Player: For those who excel in teamwork.
Great Job: For acknowledging a job well done.
Making Work Fun: For those who bring joy to the workplace.
Amazing Mentor: For individuals who provide valuable guidance.
Outside the Box Thinker: For those who showcase creativity.
Great Presentation: For individuals who deliver excellent presentations.
Making an Impact: For those who significantly influence their environment.

Advantages of Giving Kudos

Strengthening Relationships: Giving kudos fosters goodwill and strengthens professional relationships; it's like creating a positive atmosphere at your party where everyone feels appreciated and valued.

Boosting Morale: Recognising others can boost their morale and motivation. Just as cheering for a friend on the dance floor encourages them to keep going, kudos can inspire colleagues to continue their great work.

Enhancing Visibility: When you give kudos, it can increase visibility for both you and the recipient. This is like spotlighting a talented dancer, drawing attention to their skills and encouraging others to join in.

Building a Positive Culture: Regularly giving kudos contributes to a positive workplace culture; it's akin to creating a fun and welcoming party atmosphere where everyone feels included and celebrated.

K

KUDOS

How Business Owners Can Use Kudos as Part of Their Strategy

1. Recognise Team Achievements

Use kudos to acknowledge team accomplishments and individual contributions. This practice can enhance team cohesion and motivation, similar to celebrating a successful party with all your guests.

2. Encourage Peer Recognition

Foster a culture where employees feel empowered to give kudos to one another. This is like encouraging guests at your party to compliment each other, creating a supportive environment.

3. Highlight Company Values

Align the types of kudos given with your company values. For example, if teamwork is a core value, emphasise the 'Team Player' kudos. This reinforces the behaviours you want to promote within your organisation.

4. Share on Company Pages

Post about the kudos given on your company's LinkedIn™ page to showcase a culture of appreciation. This is like sharing photos and highlights from your party, showcasing the fun and engagement that took place.

5. Incorporate into Performance Reviews

Use kudos as part of performance evaluations to highlight positive contributions. This can help create a more holistic view of an employee's impact, similar to recognising the best moments from your party when reflecting on its success.

Giving kudos on LinkedIn™ is a powerful way to recognise and appreciate the contributions of others in your professional network, much like giving a heartfelt toast at your party to celebrate a friend's amazing successes. By incorporating kudos into your business strategy, you can strengthen relationships, boost morale, and foster a positive workplace culture. So, get ready to raise your glass and celebrate the achievements of your colleagues, creating an uplifting atmosphere that resonates throughout your professional community, just like the infectious joy that fills the dance floor at a great party.

K

KUDOS

Kudos, Endorsements, and Recommendations compared

Kudos: The Party Shout-Out

Kudos on LinkedIn™ are like giving someone a public shout-out at a party. This is a quick, fun way to acknowledge someone's efforts or achievements. Imagine grabbing the microphone and saying, "Hey everyone, let's hear it for John who just landed a big client!" It's visible to everyone at the party (your network) but is more of a fleeting moment of recognition.

Endorsements: The Party Small Talk

Endorsements are similar to casual compliments you might give during party small talk. It's like saying, "Hey, I heard you're great at project management", as you pass someone at the buffet. They're quick, easy to give, and accumulate over time. However, they don't carry as much weight as more substantial forms of recognition.

Recommendations: The Heartfelt Toast

Recommendations are like giving a heartfelt toast at the party. They require more effort and thought, much like preparing a speech to honour someone. When you give a recommendation, you're taking the time to craft a meaningful message about someone's skills and character; it's more impactful and carries more weight.

Key Differences:

1. *Depth:* Kudos are quick and casual, endorsements are slightly more specific but still brief, while recommendations are in-depth and detailed.
2. *Visibility:* Kudos appear in the feed temporarily, endorsements show up on profiles as skill validations, and recommendations are prominently displayed on profiles.
3. *Effort:* Kudos take seconds to give, endorsements are just a click, but recommendations require time and thought to write.
4. *Impact:* Recommendations generally carry the most weight, followed by endorsements, with kudos being more of a friendly gesture.
5. *Permanence:* Kudos are transient, endorsements accumulate over time, and recommendations remain on profiles unless removed.

CHOICE POINTS

To learn more about recommendations, turn to page 141.

• To explore more about endorsements, turn to page 45.

• To find out more about direct messaging, turn to page 42.

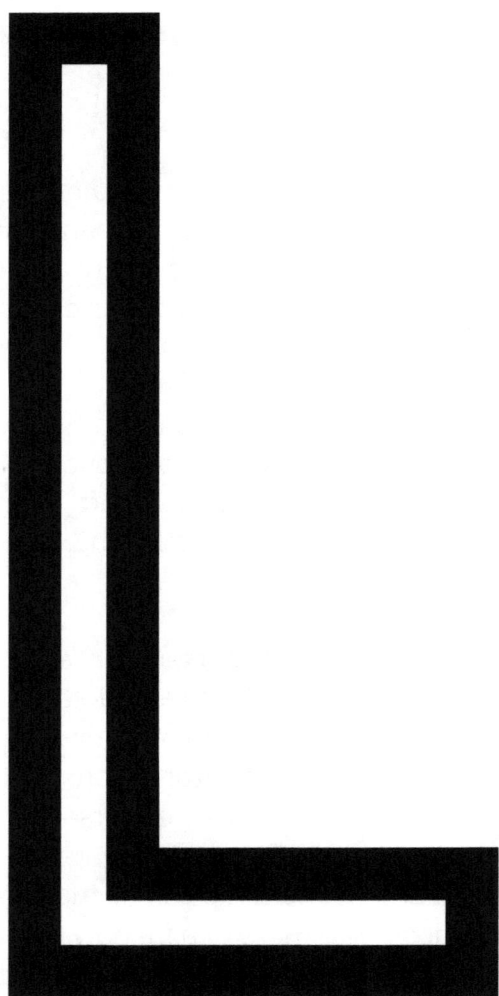

L

37. LEAD GENERATION

Imagine your disco party is the hottest event in town, and you want to make sure the right people know about it and show up. Lead generation on LinkedIn™ is like sending out exclusive invites to potential guests who would love your party; it's about attracting and engaging the right audience to grow your business.

Lead generation on LinkedIn™ is crucial because it helps you connect with potential clients, partners, and collaborators. Just like inviting the right crowd to your party ensures a lively atmosphere, generating quality leads ensures your business thrives with the right opportunities.

How Does Lead Generation Work on LinkedIn®?

Lead generation on LinkedIn™ involves several strategies to attract and engage potential clients. Here's how it works:

Optimise Your Profile

Your LinkedIn™ profile is like the entrance to your party. Make sure it's welcoming and showcases your expertise. Use a professional photo, a compelling headline, and a detailed summary to make a strong first impression.

Share Valuable Content

Posting articles, updates, and insights relevant to your industry can attract attention; it's like playing popular songs at your party to keep the guests entertained. Ensure your content is educational and engaging to draw in your target audience.

Join Relevant Groups

Participate in LinkedIn™ groups where your potential clients are active. This is like mingling with guests at different sections of your party to build connections Share valuable insights and engage in discussions to establish your presence.

Engage with Your Network

Actively engage with your connections by commenting on their posts and sharing their content. This is like interacting with guests at your party to make them feel valued and appreciated.

L

LEAD GENERATION

What Should Be Included in Your Lead-Generation Strategy?

To make your lead-generation efforts effective, include the following elements:

Clear Value Proposition: Clearly state what you offer and how it benefits your target audience. This is like highlighting the best features of your party to entice guests.

Targeted Keywords: Use relevant keywords in your profile and content to improve searchability. This ensures that your profile shows up in searches related to your expertise, much like advertising your party with popular themes.

Engaging Visuals: Include images and videos in your posts to capture attention; it's like using vibrant decorations to make your party visually appealing.

Call to Action: Encourage your audience to take action, whether it's visiting your website, signing up for a newsletter, or contacting you directly; it's like inviting guests to join the dance floor and be part of the fun.

How Can Businesses Find the Right Leads?

Finding the right leads on LinkedIn™ involves research and strategic engagement:

Identify Your Target Audience: Define who your ideal clients are. Consider their industry, job titles, and specific needs; it's like knowing the type of guests you want at your party.

Use Advanced Search Filters: LinkedIn™ offers advanced search filters to narrow down potential leads. Use these filters to find individuals who match your criteria, similar to sending invites to specific guests.

Analyse Competitor Connections: Look at who your competitors are connected with and engage with those individuals. This is like seeing who's attending other popular parties and inviting them to yours.

Leverage Analytics: Use LinkedIn™ analytics to track the performance of your posts. This helps you understand what resonates with your audience, much like adjusting your playlist based on the crowd's reaction.

L

LEAD GENERATION

Lead generation on LinkedIn™ is like curating the perfect guest list for your disco party. By optimising your profile, sharing valuable content, engaging with your network, and using targeted ads, you can attract and connect with potential clients and partners. Implement these strategies to ensure your LinkedIn™ presence is as dynamic and engaging as the best party in town, and watch your business grow with quality leads.

CHOICE POINTS

If you want to learn more about goal setting, turn to page 208.
To explore more about strategy, turn to page 169.
To find out about finding leads, go to page 55.

DID YOU KNOW?

LinkedIn® is an especially good source for discovering leads. HubSpot found that LinkedIn® is 277 % more effective at generating leads than Facebook and X.

L

38. LINKEDIN® LEARNING

Your Path to Professional Growth

LinkedIn™ Learning is an online educational platform that offers a vast library of video courses covering a wide range of topics, from business and technology to creative skills. Think of it as a dance floor where you can learn new moves and refine your skills to shine in your professional life.

While LinkedIn™ Learning offers a free trial period for new users, it is primarily a subscription-based service. After the trial, users must pay a monthly fee to access the full range of courses. This is similar to getting a VIP pass to an exclusive party, where you have access to all the best features and experiences.

Advantages of LinkedIn® Learning

1. Diverse Course Offerings: With thousands of courses available, you can find content tailored to your specific interests and career goals; it's like having a playlist that caters to every taste at your party, ensuring there's something for everyone.

2. Expert Instructors: Courses are taught by industry professionals and experts, providing high-quality instruction. This is akin to having renowned DJs at your party, ensuring the music is top-notch and engaging.

3. Flexible Learning: You can learn at your own pace, accessing courses anytime and anywhere. This flexibility allows you to fit learning into your busy schedule, much like choosing when to hit the dance floor during the party.

4. Skill Development: LinkedIn™ Learning helps you acquire new skills and improve existing ones, making you more competitive in the job market; it's like perfecting your dance moves to stand out and impress the crowd.

L

LINKEDIN® LEARNING

5. Certificates of Completion: Upon finishing a course, you receive a certificate that you can showcase on your LinkedIn™ profile. This is similar to receiving a trophy for your dance performance, highlighting your achievements to potential employers.

6. Integration with LinkedIn™: Your learning activity is integrated into your LinkedIn™ profile, allowing connections to see your commitment to professional development. This is like sharing highlights from your party, showing others how much fun you had and what you learned.

LinkedIn™ Learning is a valuable resource for professionals looking to enhance their skills and knowledge. With its diverse course offerings, expert instructors, and flexible learning options, it provides an excellent opportunity for personal and professional growth. So, step onto the LinkedIn™ Learning dance floor, and let the rhythm of knowledge elevate your career to new heights.

CHOICE POINTS

If you want to learn more about thought leadership, turn to page 182.
To explore more about skills, turn to page 160.
To find out more about research, turn to page 149.

DID YOU KNOW?

In 2023, the most popular course was 'Excel Essential Training'. Also Courses on 'Leadership' and 'Communication' are among the top 5 most popular.

39. MARKETING ON LINKEDIN®

Your disco party is the talk of the town, and you want to make sure everyone knows about it and wants to join. Marketing on LinkedIn™ is like promoting your event to attract the right crowd, ensuring your professional presence shines and your business grows. However, it's important to remember that LinkedIn™ marketing is only effective if your target audience is active on the platform.

Marketing on LinkedIn™ is crucial because it connects you with a vast network of professionals, potential clients, and industry leaders; it's like having a megaphone to announce your party to the most influential people in town. With over 1 billion members, LinkedIn™ offers unparalleled opportunities for brand visibility and engagement, but the key is to focus on building relationships and engaging with your audience rather than merely broadcasting your message.

How Does Marketing on LinkedIn® Work?

Marketing on LinkedIn™ involves several strategies to promote your brand, products, or services effectively. Here's how it works:

Profile Optimisation
Your LinkedIn™ profile is your digital storefront. Ensure it's complete, professional, and optimised with relevant keywords. This is like decorating the entrance to your party to make it inviting and eye-catching.

Content Strategy
Share valuable content that resonates with your target audience. This includes articles, posts, videos, and infographics; it's like playing the right music to keep your guests entertained and engaged. Remember, the goal is to foster conversations and connections, not just to push out promotional messages.

LinkedIn® Ads
Use LinkedIn™'s advertising platform to create targeted ads. These can be sponsored content, text ads, or InMail messages. This is like sending personalised invitations to potential VIP guests who are interested in what you have to offer.

Engage with Your Network
Actively participate in discussions, comment on posts, and share insights. This is similar to mingling with guests at your party, making them feel valued and connected. Engagement is key, focus on building relationships rather than simply broadcasting your message.

MARKETING ON LINKEDIN®

Join and Create Groups

Participate in LinkedIn™ groups related to your industry or create your own. This is like hosting a themed section at your party where like-minded guests can interact and share ideas, fostering a sense of community.

Utilise LinkedIn® Analytics

Monitor the performance of your posts and ads using LinkedIn™ analytics. This helps you understand what works and what doesn't, just like adjusting your playlist based on the crowd's reaction.

What Should Be Included in Your LinkedIn® Marketing Strategy?

To make your LinkedIn™ marketing efforts effective, include the following elements:

Clear Objectives: Define what you want to achieve with your marketing efforts, whether it's brand awareness, lead generation, or customer engagement. This is like setting the theme and goals for your party.

Target Audience: Identify who you want to reach with your marketing messages. This helps tailor your content and ads to their interests and needs, just like creating a guest list for your party.

Consistent Branding: Ensure your profile and posts reflect your brand's identity. This consistency builds recognition and trust, much like having a consistent theme throughout your party.

High-Quality Content: Share content that provides value to your audience, such as industry insights, how-to guides, and success stories; it's like playing hit songs that everyone loves and talks about.

Engagement Strategy: Use polls, questions, and interactive content to engage your audience. This encourages participation, similar to hosting games or activities at your party.

MARKETING ON LINKEDIN®

Advantages of Marketing on LinkedIn®

1. Professional Audience: LinkedIn™'s user base consists of professionals and decision-makers making it ideal for B2B marketing. This is like having a guest list filled with influential people who can help your party (and business) succeed.

2. Targeted Advertising: LinkedIn™ offers advanced targeting options based on job title, industry, company size, and more. This ensures your ads reach the right people, similar to sending invites to those who will appreciate your party the most.

3. Enhanced Credibility: A strong LinkedIn™ presence enhances your brand's credibility and authority; it's like being known as the best party host in town, attracting more guests and positive attention.

4. Networking Opportunities: LinkedIn™ facilitates networking with industry leaders, potential clients, and collaborators; it's like meeting new friends at your party who can help you grow and succeed.

Marketing on LinkedIn™ is like promoting your disco party to ensure it's the hottest event in town. By optimising your profile, sharing valuable content, engaging with your network, and using targeted ads, you can effectively reach and connect with your target audience. The key is to build relationships and engage with your audience, not just to broadcast your message. Implement these strategies to make your LinkedIn™ marketing efforts as dynamic and successful as the best party in town, and watch your business thrive.

CHOICE POINTS

If you want to learn more about groups, turn to page 60.
To explore more about industry insights, turn to page 74.
If you wish to delve deeper into strategy, go to page 169.

N

40. NAME PRONUNCIATION FEATURE

The name-pronunciation feature that is often overlooked on LinkedIn™ can significantly enhance your professional profile. Just as a disco party thrives on the right atmosphere and personal touches, correctly pronouncing your name can add a layer of authenticity and personality to your online presence.

Here's how business owners can use this feature to promote their business and the benefits it brings.

What is Name Pronunciation?
LinkedIn™ allows users to record a short audio clip (ten seconds) of their name pronunciation, making it easier for others to hear how to say it correctly. This feature is particularly beneficial for individuals with unique or complex names, helping to foster better communication and connection. Think of it as the DJ introducing themselves on the mic, ensuring everyone knows who's behind the decks and setting the tone for the night.

Why Should Business Owners Use Name Pronunciation?

Enhances Personal Connection
By providing a clear pronunciation of your name, you make it easier for others to address you correctly. This fosters a sense of connection and respect, akin to how a DJ makes an effort to engage with the crowd, creating a welcoming atmosphere. When people feel they can pronounce your name correctly, it builds rapport and trust.

Promotes Inclusivity
Using the name pronunciation feature shows that you value diversity and inclusivity; it acknowledges that names can carry cultural significance and that everyone deserves to be addressed correctly. This is similar to a disco party where the DJ celebrates different music styles, making everyone feel included and appreciated.

Adds Personality to Your Profile
A recorded pronunciation adds a personal touch to your LinkedIn™ profile, allowing your personality to shine through. Just as a DJ's unique style and flair can elevate a party, your voice can convey warmth and approachability, making your profile more memorable.

N

NAME PRONUNCIATION FEATURE

Strengthens Brand Identity

For business owners, having a clear and engaging name pronunciation can reinforce brand identity. It helps to create a cohesive image across all platforms, much like the way a DJ's brand is built on their music style and performance. When potential clients hear your name pronounced confidently, it can leave a lasting impression.

Facilitates Networking

When you connect with others, especially in professional settings, having your name pronounced correctly can make networking smoother; it's like a DJ seamlessly transitioning between tracks, keeping the energy flowing and the crowd engaged. Ensuring that people can say your name correctly can lead to more meaningful connections and opportunities.

What can you say in 10 seconds?

Ten seconds is approximately 23 words, depending on how fast you speak. So you can use the name pronunciation feature to say an abridged version of your headline or talk about your current offer or promotion.

Using the name pronunciation feature on LinkedIn™ is a powerful way for business owners to promote their personal brand, enhance connections, and add personality to their profiles. By ensuring that others can pronounce your name correctly, you foster inclusivity and respect, creating a welcoming professional environment. Just as a DJ creates an unforgettable atmosphere at a disco party, your name pronunciation can leave a lasting impression on your network. Embrace this feature and watch as it enhances your LinkedIn™ presence and strengthens your professional relationships.

CHOICE POINTS

If you want to learn more about building your brand, turn to page 21.
To explore more about optimisation, turn to page 117.
To find out about using new features, go to page 103.

N

41. NETWORKING

Your disco party is filled with vibrant conversations, laughter, and connections being made. Networking on LinkedIn™ is just like that; it's about building relationships, exchanging ideas, and creating opportunities that can benefit your professional journey. Networking on LinkedIn™ is essential because it allows you to connect with industry professionals, potential clients, and collaborators. Just as mingling with guests at your party can lead to new friendships and partnerships, networking on LinkedIn™ opens doors to valuable opportunities and insights. Here's how it works:

Optimise Your Profile
Ensure your LinkedIn™ profile is complete and professional. This is like having an inviting entrance to your party that encourages guests to come in and mingle. A well-crafted profile makes a strong first impression.

Engage with Content
Actively comment on and share posts from your connections and industry leaders. This is akin to participating in conversations at your party, showing that you're interested and engaged.

Send Personalised Connection Requests
When reaching out to new connections, include a personalised message explaining why you want to connect; it's like introducing yourself to someone at the party and sharing a bit about why you'd like to get to know them better.

Join Relevant Groups
Participate in LinkedIn™ groups related to your field. This is like creating a special area at your party where guests with similar interests can gather and share ideas.

Attend LinkedIn® Events
Look for webinars, workshops, and networking events hosted on LinkedIn™. These events provide opportunities to meet new people and learn from experts, similar to hosting a fun activity at your party to encourage interaction.

Follow Up
After connecting with someone, send a follow-up message to thank them and suggest a conversation. This is like following up with guests after the party to keep the connection alive.

N

NETWORKING

Benefits of Networking on LinkedIn®

1. Access to Opportunities: Networking can lead to new business opportunities, partnerships, and collaborations. This is like meeting someone at your party who introduces you to a new opportunity you hadn't considered.

2. Knowledge Sharing: Engaging with others allows you to share insights and learn from their experiences. This is like exchanging stories and tips with fellow party-goers, enriching your own knowledge.

3. Increased Visibility: Active networking increases your profile's visibility, making it easier for others to find you; it's like being the life of the party, drawing attention and interest from guests.

4. Building Relationships: Networking fosters meaningful connections that can lead to long-term professional relationships. Just as friendships formed at a party can last well beyond the event, connections made on LinkedIn™ can lead to fruitful collaborations.

Networking on LinkedIn™ is like creating a vibrant atmosphere at your disco party where connections flourish and opportunities arise. By optimising your profile, engaging with content, sending personalised connection requests, and participating in groups and events, you can build a strong professional network that supports your career growth. So, get ready to dance your way through LinkedIn™, making valuable connections and enjoying the benefits of a robust professional network.

CHOICE POINTS

If you want to learn more about optimisation, turn to page 117.
To explore more about finding leads, turn to page 55.
To find out more about referrals, go to page 144.

N

42. NEW FEATURES

Imagine your disco party is constantly evolving with new themes, exciting performances, and fresh music to keep the energy high. Keeping up with new features on LinkedIn™ is just like that; it ensures your professional presence remains dynamic and relevant in a rapidly changing digital landscape.

Staying updated with LinkedIn™'s new features is crucial for several reasons:

Enhanced Functionality
New features often provide additional tools and capabilities that can improve your networking and marketing efforts. Just as new lighting or sound systems can elevate the atmosphere of your party, these features can enhance your LinkedIn™ experience.

Competitive Advantage
Being aware of the latest updates allows you to leverage new tools before your competitors do. This is like to being the first to introduce a trending dance move at your party, making you the centre of attention.

Improved Engagement
New features often encourage more interaction and engagement among users. By utilising these tools, you can foster deeper connections, just like introducing fun games or activities that get your guests mingling.

Optimised Profile Visibility
LinkedIn™ frequently updates its algorithms and features that affect how profiles are displayed in searches. Staying informed helps you optimise your profile accordingly, ensuring you remain visible to potential connections and opportunities.

Better Networking Opportunities
New features can introduce innovative ways to connect with others, such as enhanced messaging options or virtual events. This is like creating new spaces at your party where guests can meet and interact.

Skill Development
LinkedIn™ often rolls out features that support professional development, such as LinkedIn Learning courses or new content-sharing options. Keeping up with these can help you continuously improve your skills, much like learning new dance routines to keep your moves fresh.

N

NEW FEATURES

How to Stay Updated

Follow LinkedIn™ Updates: Regularly check LinkedIn™'s official blog or help centre for announcements about new features and updates. This is like keeping an eye on the latest music trends to ensure your party playlist is always current.

Engage with Your Network: Discuss new features with your connections and learn how they're using them. This interaction can provide insights and tips, similar to sharing party-planning ideas with fellow hosts.

Participate in Webinars and Workshops: Attend LinkedIn™-hosted events that focus on new features and best practices. These events can provide valuable information and networking opportunities, much like attending industry conferences to learn about the latest trends.

Experiment with New Tools: Don't hesitate to try out new features as they become available. Hands-on experience is the best way to understand how they can benefit you, just like testing out a new dance floor layout before the party starts.

Keeping up with new features on LinkedIn™ is essential for maintaining a vibrant and engaging professional presence. By staying informed and adapting to changes, you can enhance your networking efforts, improve your visibility, and gain a competitive edge in your industry. So, get ready to embrace the latest updates on LinkedIn™ and ensure your professional journey is as dynamic and exciting as the best disco party in town.

CHOICE POINTS

If you want to learn more about engagement, turn to page 46.
To explore more about experimentation, turn to page 204.
To find out about the algorithm, go to page 6.

N

43. NEWSFEED

Imagine your disco party is alive with energy, where the music sets the mood and the conversations flow freely. The LinkedIn™ newsfeed is much like that vibrant atmosphere; it's where you engage with your network, share insights, and stay updated on industry trends. Keeping up with your newsfeed is essential for maintaining an active and relevant professional presence. Here's how it works:

Real-Time Updates
The newsfeed provides real-time updates from your connections, industry leaders, and companies you follow. This is like the latest hits playing at your party, keeping the energy high and the conversations fresh.

Engagement Opportunities
It allows you to engage with content shared by your network, fostering discussions and building relationships. Just as mingling with guests at your party creates connections, interacting with posts can strengthen your professional ties.

Showcasing Expertise
By sharing your own insights and content, you can position yourself as a thought leader in your industry. This is like taking the stage at your party to showcase your best dance moves, drawing attention and admiration.

Staying Informed
The newsfeed keeps you informed about industry trends, news, and updates. This knowledge is crucial for making informed decisions and staying competitive, much like knowing the latest dance trends to keep your party exciting.

Networking Potential
Engaging with posts can lead to new connections and opportunities. Commenting on a shared article, or liking a colleague's post, can spark conversations that may lead to collaborations, similar to meeting new friends at your party.

N

NEWSFEED

How to Effectively Use the Newsfeed

Engage Regularly: Make it a habit to check your newsfeed daily and engage with posts that resonate with you. Commenting, liking, and sharing content helps keep your network active and engaged, just like encouraging guests to dance and interact at your party.

Share Valuable Content: Post articles, insights, and updates that showcase your expertise and interests. This is like sharing the best music at your party, ensuring everyone enjoys the experience and remembers it.

Follow Industry Leaders: Connect with and follow industry leaders to gain insights and updates from the forefront of your field. This is like inviting influential DJs to your party, ensuring the music is top-notch and relevant.

Utilise Hashtags: When posting, use relevant hashtags to increase the visibility of your content. This helps attract like-minded professionals to your posts, similar to using catchy themes to draw in guests.

Participate in Discussions: Join conversations in the comments section of posts to share your thoughts and insights. This engagement can lead to deeper connections and collaborations, much like networking with guests during a lively discussion at your party.

The LinkedIn™ newsfeed is a vital component of your professional presence, much like the lively atmosphere at your disco party. By staying engaged with your newsfeed, sharing valuable content, and participating in discussions, you can enhance your networking efforts and position yourself as a thought leader in your industry. So, keep the energy high, stay informed, and make the most of your LinkedIn™ newsfeed to ensure your professional journey is as dynamic and exciting as the best party in town.

CHOICE POINTS

If you want to learn more about hashtags, turn to page 65.

To explore more about trending topics, go to page 184.

For more information regarding notifications, go to page 110.

N

44. NEWSLETTERS

Imagine your disco party has a VIP mailing list that keeps guests informed about upcoming events and exclusive offers. LinkedIn™ newsletters serve a similar purpose for your professional network, helping you grow your business and build your own list of engaged followers. Here's how it works:

Increased Visibility

Newsletters appear in subscribers' notifications, email inboxes, and newsfeeds, increasing your content's visibility; it's like sending out VIP invitations that ensure your most interested guests never miss a party.

Thought Leadership

Regular newsletters establish you as an authority in your field. This is like being known as the go-to host for the best-themed parties in town.

Audience Engagement

Newsletters foster ongoing engagement with your network, keeping your brand top-of-mind; it's like maintaining excitement between events by sharing sneak peeks and highlights.

Lead Generation

By providing valuable content, you can attract potential clients and partners. This is similar to offering exclusive perks to VIP guests, encouraging them to bring friends to future events.

How to Grow Your Own List Using LinkedIn® Newsletters

While LinkedIn™ doesn't provide direct access to subscribers' email addresses, you can leverage newsletters to grow your own list:

1. Provide Exclusive Content: Offer newsletter-only insights or resources that entice readers to seek more; it's like giving VIP guests a taste of an exclusive experience, making them eager for the full party.

2. Include Clear CTAs: In each newsletter, include a call to action (CTA) that directs readers to your website or landing page where they can sign up to your email list. This is similar to offering VIP guests a special pass for future events if they register on your guest list.

N

NEWSLETTERS

3. Tease Additional Content: Mention expanded versions of articles or exclusive offers available only to your email subscribers; it's like hinting at an afterparty that's only open to those on your personal guest list.

4. Host 'Gated' Content: Direct readers to valuable resources on your website that require an email sign up to access. This is like offering VIP guests access to a special lounge at your party if they RSVP with their contact details.

5. Promote Your Email Newsletter: Use your LinkedIn™ newsletter to promote your separate email newsletter, highlighting its unique benefits. This is like announcing an exclusive event series that's only open to your most dedicated fans.

6. Engage in Comments: Respond to comments on your newsletter and guide interested readers to your website or email list for more in-depth discussions. This personal touch is like chatting with guests at your party and inviting them to smaller, more intimate gatherings.

Best Practices for LinkedIn® Newsletters

<u>Choose a Relevant Name:</u> Select a newsletter name that clearly describes your theme, making it easy for your audience to understand its value.

<u>Maintain Consistency:</u> Stick to a regular publishing schedule to keep your audience engaged.

<u>Provide Value:</u> Share practical tips, insights, and industry news to keep your content relevant and useful.

<u>Optimise for Engagement:</u> Use compelling headlines, ask questions, and encourage discussions to boost engagement.

LinkedIn™ newsletters are a powerful tool for growing your business and building your own list. By providing valuable content, strategically guiding readers to your website, and following best practices, you can use your LinkedIn™ newsletter as a stepping stone to expand your reach and nurture a dedicated audience. So, start planning your newsletter strategy and watch your professional network grow like the guest list for the hottest party in town.

N

CHOICE POINTS

If you want to learn more about visibility, turn to page 197.

To explore more about generating leads, turn to page 89.

To find out about thought leadership, go to page 182.

DID YOU KNOW?

According to THM there are over 63,000 newsletters on LinkedIn® and when it comes to publishing frequency, the weekly publishing schedule is the most popular at 45%.

N

45. NOTIFICATIONS

Your disco party is filled with excitement, and you have a system in place to keep guests updated about special performances, surprise guests, or important announcements. Notifications on LinkedIn™ serve a similar purpose, they keep you informed about relevant activities, helping you engage with your network and stay connected. Here's how they work:

Timely Updates
Notifications alert you to important activities such as connection requests, comments on your posts, mentions, and new followers. This is like receiving real-time updates at your party, ensuring you're aware of what's happening and can engage accordingly.

Engagement Opportunities
By responding to notifications, you can engage with your network more effectively. Just as you would interact with guests who approach you at your party, engaging with notifications helps build and strengthen relationships.

Content Visibility
Notifications can increase the visibility of your posts and articles as interactions from your network can lead to more engagement. This is like announcing a particularly exciting moment at your party, drawing more attention and participation.

Networking Potential
Notifications about job changes, work anniversaries, or shared content from your connections, provide opportunities to reach out and reconnect. This is similar to noticing when a guest has brought a friend to your party, giving you a chance to introduce yourself and expand your circle.

Types of Notifications on LinkedIn®

1.*Connection Requests:* Alerts you when someone wants to connect, allowing you to expand your network.

2.*Engagement Notifications:* Alerts when someone likes, comments on, or shares your posts, prompting you to engage back.

N

NOTIFICATIONS

3.Mentions: Notifications when someone tags you in a post or comment, inviting you to join the conversation.

4.Profile Views: Notifications about who has viewed your profile, giving you insight into who might be interested in connecting.

How to Manage Notifications Effectively

Custom se Your Settings: Adjust your notification settings to receive alerts that matter most to you. This is like choosing which announcements to make at your party to keep the focus on what's most important.

Engage Promptly: Respond to notifications in a timely manner to show appreciation and foster connections. Just as you would greet guests promptly, engaging quickly helps maintain momentum in your professional relationships.

Prioritise Meaningful Interactions: Focus on notifications that lead to meaningful conversations or opportunities; it's like prioritising interactions with guests who bring energy and excitement to your party.

Use Notifications for Follow-ups: Use engagement notifications as a reason to reconnect with contacts. For example, if someone comments on your post, follow up with a message to thank them and continue the conversation.

Stay Informed: Regularly check your notifications to stay updated on industry news and trends shared by your connections. This keeps you informed and allows you to contribute to discussions, much like staying aware of the latest dance moves to keep the party lively.

Utilise the bell notification: When you click the bell icon on someone's profile, you ensure that you receive notifications every time they share new content. This is especially important for keeping up with industry experts who can provide valuable insights and updates that keep you ahead of the game. Just as a party-goer who knows the hottest tracks can keep the energy alive, staying connected with industry leaders allows you to tap into the latest trends and discussions shaping your field.

N

NOTIFICATIONS

Notifications on LinkedIn™ are essential for staying engaged and informed within your professional network. By managing your notifications effectively, you can seize opportunities for interaction, strengthen relationships, and enhance your visibility. So, keep an eye on those notifications, engage with your network, and ensure your LinkedIn™ presence is as vibrant and dynamic as the best disco party in town.

CHOICE POINTS

If you want to learn more about bell notifications, turn to page 19.
To explore more about privacy settings, turn to page 134.
To find out about tags and mentions, go to page 174.

TOP TIP

To maximise your visibility and engagement on LinkedIn®, encourage your connections to click the bell notification on your profile. This feature is like having a personal spotlight at a party, ensuring that your updates shine brightly and are seen by those who matter most.

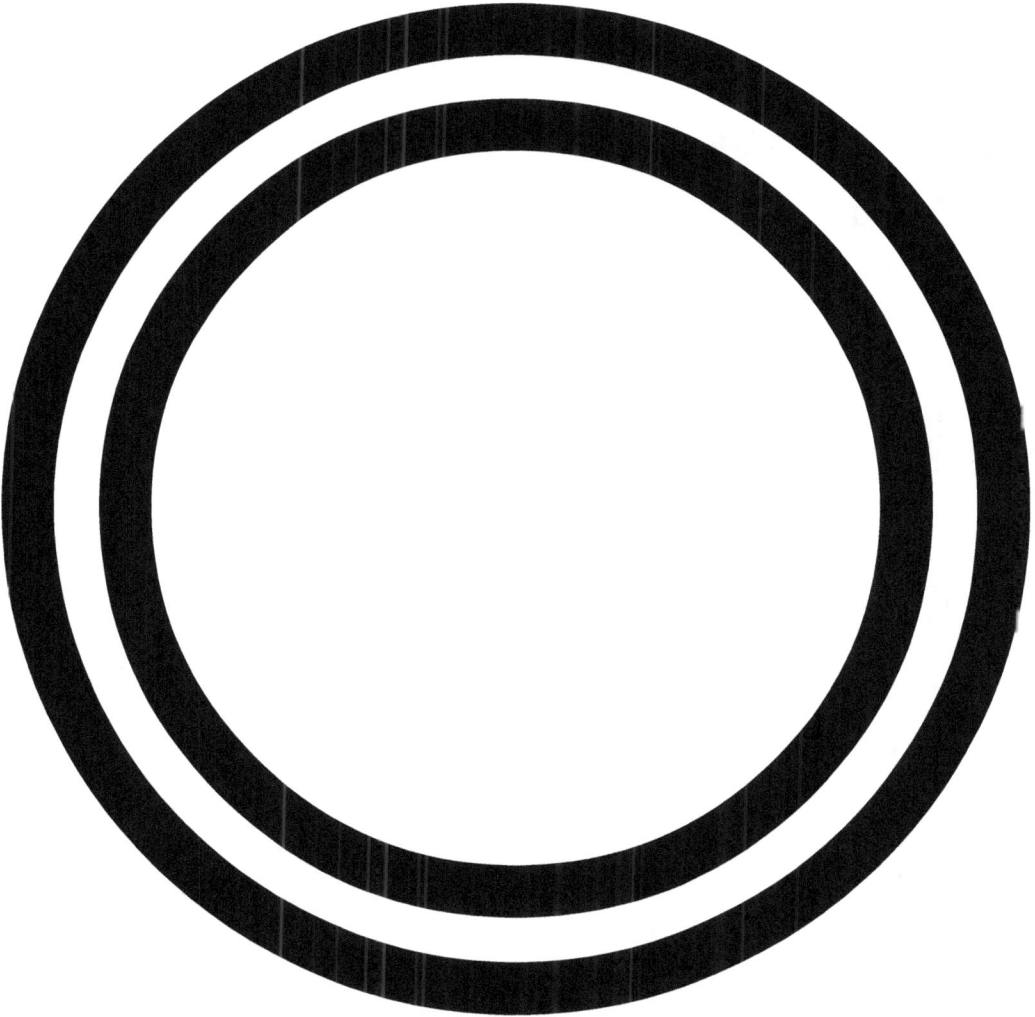

46. 'OPEN TO WORK' FRAME

The 'Open to Work' frame on LinkedIn™ profile photos is a feature that has sparked debate among professionals. Like choosing the perfect outfit for your disco party, deciding whether to use this frame requires careful consideration.

For business owners and freelancers, deciding whether to use this frame involves weighing up the potential benefits and drawbacks.

Advantages of Using the 'Open to Work' Frame:

1. Increased Visibility
The frame makes your profile stand out, potentially increasing your chances of being noticed; it's like wearing a distinctive outfit at a networking event, ensuring you catch people's attention.

2. Clear Signal
It clearly communicates your availability for new opportunities, eliminating any ambiguity. This is like openly stating your intentions at a business mixer, making it easier for others to understand your current status.

3. Networking Opportunities
The frame can prompt your network to make introductions. Just as party-goers might introduce you to new contacts if they know you're looking, your LinkedIn™ connections might be more inclined to help.

5. Empowerment and Confidence
Openly declaring you are 'open to work' can be empowering and demonstrate a proactive approach to business development; it projects confidence and initiative, which can be attractive traits to potential clients.

Disadvantages of Using the 'Open to Work' Frame:

1. Potential Stigma
Some argue that it can make you appear desperate which might deter some clients. This is similar to appearing too eager at a networking event, which might put off potential business partners.

'OPEN TO WORK' FRAME

2. Overuse
With many people using the frame, it might lose its effectiveness in making you stand out; if everyone at the event is wearing the same badge, it no longer helps you.

3. Potential Bias
Some businesses might have preconceived notions about individuals using the frame, potentially leading to unconscious bias. This is like being judged for using a particular approach at a networking event - some might appreciate it, while others might be put off.

The decision to use the 'Open to Work' frame on your LinkedIn™ profile photo is a personal one that depends on your specific circumstances. For business owners and freelancers, it can be a useful tool to increase visibility and signal availability, but it also comes with potential drawbacks that need to be carefully considered. Like choosing the perfect outfit for a party, it's about finding the right balance between standing out and maintaining a professional image. Consider your industry norms and personal comfort level when making this decision. Remember, there are other ways to signal your openness to new opportunities on LinkedIn™ that might be more subtle yet effective.

CHOICE POINTS

If you want to learn more about hiring, turn to page 69.

To explore more about visibility, turn to page 197.

To find out more about lead generation, go to page 89.

47. OPTIMISATION

Optimising your LinkedIn™ profile is like fine-tuning your disco party to ensure it's the hottest event in town; it's about making your professional presence as engaging and effective as possible to attract the right opportunities and connections. Hers's how it works:

Increased Visibility
An optimised profile appears higher in LinkedIn™ search results, making you more discoverable to potential employers, clients, or collaborators. This is like having your party featured at the top of the local event listings.

Better First Impressions
A well-optimised profile creates a strong first impression, showcasing your skills and experience effectively. This is like having an impressive entrance to your disco that wows guests as soon as they arrive.

Targeted Networking
By using relevant keywords and highlighting specific skills, you attract connections that align with your professional goals; it's like tailoring your party theme to attract the crowd you want.

Key Elements of LinkedIn® Profile Optimisation:

1. *Professional Photo:* Use a high-quality, professional headshot. This is your virtual handshake, like greeting guests at your party with a warm smile.

2. *Compelling Headline:* Craft a headline that goes beyond your job title, highlighting your unique value proposition. This is like having an eye-catching banner at your party entrance.

3. *About section:* Write a concise yet comprehensive summary that tells your professional story. Think of it as the opening speech at your party, setting the tone for the entire event.

OPTIMISATION

4. Relevant Keywords: Incorporate industry-specific keywords throughout your profile to improve searchability. This is like using popular music genres to attract the right crowd to your disco.

5. Detailed Experience Section: Provide comprehensive information about your work history, focusing on achievements rather than just responsibilities; it's like showcasing your best dance moves to impress the crowd.

6. Skills and Endorsements: List relevant skills and seek endorsements from colleagues. This is like having VIPs vouch for your party's quality.

7. Recommendations: Request and provide recommendations to build credibility; it's like having satisfied partygoers leave glowing reviews about your event.

8. Multimedia Content: Include relevant articles, presentations, or videos to showcase your work. This is similar to having various entertainment options at your party to keep guests engaged.

Best Practices for Profile Optimisation:

Regular Updates: Keep your profile current, adding new skills, experiences, and achievements; it's like constantly refreshing your party playlist to keep it exciting.

Engage Actively: Regularly share content, comment on posts, and participate in group discussions. This increases your visibility, much like being an active host who mingles with all the guests.

Customise Your URL: Create a custom LinkedIn™ URL for easier sharing and improved SEO (Search Engine Optimization). This is like having a catchy, easy to remember name for your party venue.

Use LinkedIn™ Features: Utilise features like Skills Assessments to further enhance your profile. This is like using special effects or unique themes to make your party stand out.

OPTIMISATION

Optimising your LinkedIn™ profile is an ongoing process that requires attention and regular updates. By focusing on these key elements and best practices, you can create a profile that not only attracts attention but also effectively showcases your professional brand. Remember, your LinkedIn™ profile is your digital stage; make sure it's set up to give your best performance.

CHOICE POINTS

If you want to learn more about keywords, turn to page 83.
To explore more about building a brand, turn to page 21.
To find out more about visibility, go to page 197.

DID YOU KNOW?

There are over 1 billion LinkedIn® users, and according to Ruben Hassid only 1% have a fully optimised profile. Research conducted by Princeton psychologists found that it takes only 1/10th of a second to form a first impression.
Your LinkedIn® profile is your first impression.
Make it count.

P

48. PERSONAL PROFILE

Your personal profile on LinkedIn™ is like your digital business card and the main stage at your disco party. This is where you showcase who you are, what you do, and how you can connect with others in your professional network. A well-crafted personal profile is essential for making a strong impression and engaging effectively with your audience.

Why is a Personal Profile Important?

First Impressions Matter

Your LinkedIn™ profile is often the first point of contact for potential partners, clients, or collaborators. A polished profile creates a positive first impression, much like a warm welcome at your party.

Showcase Your Expertise

Your personal profile allows you to highlight your skills, experiences, and achievements, establishing your credibility in your field, much like showcasing your best dance moves to impress the crowd.

Networking Opportunities

A strong personal profile helps you connect with like-minded professionals and industry leaders; it's like having an inviting atmosphere at your party that encourages guests to mingle and network.

Advancement

An optimised personal profile can lead to collaborations, and new opportunities; it's similar to how a successful party can lead to future invitations and partnerships.

Key Components of a Personal Profile

1. Professional Photo: Use a high-quality, approachable headshot. This is your virtual handshake, setting the tone for how others perceive you.

2. Compelling Headline: Craft a headline that reflects your current role, skills, and what you bring to the table. This should be more than just your job title; think of it as an enticing tagline for your party.

3. Engaging Summary: Write a summary that tells your professional story, highlighting your passions, skills, and career goals. This is like the opening speech at your party, inviting guests to learn more about you.

P

PERSONAL PROFILE

4. Detailed Experience Section: List your work history with a focus on achievements and contributions rather than just duties. This showcases your impact, similar to how you'd highlight the best moments of your party.

5. Skills and Endorsements: Include relevant skills and seek endorsements from colleagues and connections. This builds credibility, much like having testimonials from satisfied party-goers.

6. Recommendations: Request recommendations from former colleagues or clients to enhance your profile's credibility; it's like having friends vouch for your party-planning skills.

7. Multimedia Content: Add articles, presentations, podcasts, or videos that showcase your work and expertise, much like providing entertainment options at your party to keep guests engaged.

8. Contact Information: Make it easy for others to reach out to you by including appropriate contact details. This is like having a clear way for guests to RSVP or ask questions about your party.

Best Practices for Maintaining Your Personal Profile

<u>Regular Updates</u>: Keep your profile current by adding new experiences, skills, and achievements. This ensures that your profile reflects your most recent professional journey, similar to refreshing your party playlist.

<u>Engage with Your Network:</u> Actively participate in discussions, share relevant content, and comment on others' posts. This interaction keeps your profile visible and fosters connections, much like mingling with guests at your party.

<u>Customise Your LinkedIn™ URL:</u> Create a custom URL for your profile to make t easier to share and improve your professional branding; it's like having a catchy name for your party that guests will remember.

<u>Utilise LinkedIn™ Features:</u> Take advantage of features such as LinkedIn Learning and Skills Assessments to enhance your profile and showcase your commitment to professional development.

P

PERSONAL PROFILE
6 Ways to Optimise Your Personal Profile

1. Know Your Audience: Just like you wouldn't throw a party without knowing who you're inviting, identify your ideal audience. Tailor your posts and content to resonate with this specific group, ensuring that your message hits home and keeps them engaged.

2. Choose the Right Profile Picture: Your profile picture is like the welcome mat at your party. It should be inviting and friendly. Use a clear, high-quality image where you're smiling and approachable, making guests feel comfortable to connect with you.

3. Craft a Memorable Headline: Your headline is the catchy party theme that grabs attention. Make it concise and impactful, clearly stating what you do and the value you offer, so guests know exactly what to expect when they arrive.

4. Design an Eye-Catching Banner: Think of your banner as the decorations that set the mood for your party. Use it to convey your brand and include a clear call-to-action, making it easy for guests to understand what you're all about.

5. Tell Your Story in the About Section: The About section is your chance to share the story behind the party. Use it to connect with your audience on a deeper level, explaining who you are, what you do, and how you can help them.

6. Showcase Your Offers in the Featured Section: This is like the highlight reel of your party, showcasing the best moments. Use the Featured section to display your services, links to your calendar, or any important content that potential clients should see first.

Your personal profile on LinkedIn™ is a vital tool for building your professional brand and connecting with others in your industry. By focusing on key components and best practices, you can create a compelling profile that effectively showcases your skills and experiences. Remember, your LinkedIn™ profile is your digital stage, make sure it's set for a standout performance that attracts the right audience and opportunities.

CHOICE POINTS

If you want to learn more about all-star profile, turn to page 8.
To explore more about URL customisation, turn to page 190.
To find out about optimisation, go to page 117.

P

49. POLLS

Polls on LinkedIn™ are an interactive feature that allows users to create and participate in surveys, gathering opinions and insights from their network. This tool can be a valuable addition to your LinkedIn™ strategy, especially if you are looking to engage your audience and gain feedback.

Why Are Polls Important?

Engagement Boost
Polls encourage interaction from your network, increasing engagement on your posts, much like hosting a fun activity at your disco party that gets everyone involved and talking.

Gathering Insights
Polls provide a quick and effective way to gather opinions and insights on specific topics. This feedback can inform your business decisions, much like asking guests for their favourite songs to play at your party.

Building Community
Polls foster a sense of community by inviting your connections to share their thoughts. This interaction can strengthen relationships, in the same way that shared activities at a party create bonds among guests.

Content Variety
Incorporating polls into your content strategy adds variety, keeping your audience engaged; it's like mixing up the music at your party to keep the atmosphere lively and exciting.

Showcasing Expertise
By asking questions related to your industry, you can position yourself as a thought leader and engage in meaningful discussions. This is akin to leading a conversation about the latest trends in music at your disco.

P

POLLS

How to Effectively Use Polls on LinkedIn®:

1. *Choose Relevant Topics*: Select topics that resonate with your audience and are relevant to your industry. This ensures that the poll is engaging and encourages participation.

2. *Keep It Simple:* Design polls that are straightforward and easy to understand. Complicated questions may deter participation, much like a confusing party invitation that leaves guests unsure of what to expect.

3. *Encourage Participation:* Promote your poll through your network and encourage connections to share their opinions. You can also follow up with a post discussing the results to keep the conversation going.

4. *Use Visuals:* Incorporate images or graphics to make your poll more visually appealing, much like using vibrant decorations at your party to attract attention.

5. *Share Results:* After the poll concludes, share the results with your network. This transparency shows that you value their input and fosters a sense of community.

6. *Engage with Comments:* Respond to comments and engage with participants to deepen connections. This interaction is like mingling with guests at your party, making them feel valued and appreciated.

Best Practices for Polls:

Limit Options: Keep the number of response options manageable (typically 2-4) to avoid overwhelming participants.

Timing Matters: Post polls when your audience is most active to maximise participation. This is like choosing the right time to play a popular song that gets everyone on the dance floor.

Promote Discussion: Encourage participants to elaborate on their choices in the comments section, fostering deeper conversations.

P

POLLS

Polls on LinkedIn™ are a powerful tool for engaging your audience, gathering insights, and building community. By incorporating polls into your content strategy, you can enhance your visibility, foster meaningful interactions, and position yourself as a thought leader in your industry. Get ready to create engaging polls that not only entertain but also inform, making your LinkedIn™ presence as dynamic and exciting as the best disco party in town.

CHOICE POINTS

If you want to learn more about research, turn to page 149.
To explore more about industry insights, turn to page 74.
To delve deeper into thought leadership, go to page 182.

TOP TIP
Keep It Simple.
Just like a fun party game, your poll should be easy to understand and quick to answer. Avoid complex questions that might confuse your audience.

P

50. POSTS

Think of LinkedIn™ posts as the vibrant dance floor at your disco party, where the energy is high, and connections are made. Each type of post serves as a different aspect of the party, inviting your audience to engage, share, and connect. Understanding the various types of posts and how to use them effectively can help you create an electrifying atmosphere that keeps everyone coming back for more.

Types of LinkedIn® Posts:

Text Posts
Short, text-only updates that share quick insights, tips, or questions. Think of these as the opening announcements at your party, setting the mood and getting everyone excited.

Image Posts
Posts that include a single image or a series of images to complement the text. These are like the dazzling lights and decorations that catch the eye and draw guests in.

Video Posts
Posts featuring video content that can be more engaging and visually appealing. This is similar to the way that a live DJ performance gets everyone on the dance floor.

Document Posts
Posts that share documents like PDFs or presentations directly in the newsfeed. This is similar to the way that you might hand out flyers or brochures at your party, providing guests with valuable information.

Polls
Interactive posts that allow you to gather opinions and insights from your network. Think of these as fun games or contests at your party, encouraging participation and interaction.

Articles
Longform content published directly on LinkedIn™, similar to blog posts. These are like the main event of your party, where you showcase your best ideas and insights.

Newsletters
Newsletters on LinkedIn™ are like the exclusive VIP lounge at your party, where you share curated insights, updates, and valuable information with your most engaged guests. They provide a platform for you to connect with your audience on a deeper level, delivering consistent content that keeps them coming back for more.

P

POSTS

How to Use LinkedIn® Posts Effectively

1. Text Posts
Best for: Quick updates, sharing personal insights, or asking questions.
Tips: Keep it concise and engaging. Start with a strong hook to grab attention, just like a catchy song that gets everyone moving.

2. Image Posts
Best for: Showcasing events, infographics, or visual content.
Tips: Use high-quality images and add a descriptive caption. Visual content can increase engagement, much like vibrant decorations that enhance the party atmosphere.

3. Video Posts
Best for: Demonstrations, tutorials, or sharing dynamic content.
Tips: Keep videos short and engaging. Just as a great DJ keeps the energy high, make sure your videos are captivating and to the point. Always use captions - most people watch videos with the sound turned off.

4. Document Posts
Best for: Sharing detailed reports, presentations, or whitepapers.
Tips: Ensure documents are visually appealing and easy to read. Clear titles and summaries will help guests (your audience) understand the key points, just like a well-organised party itinerary.

5. Polls
Best for: Gathering feedback, opinions, or conducting quick surveys.
Tips: Ask relevant and straightforward questions. After the poll, share the results and follow up with a discussion to keep the engagement going, like announcing the winners of a party game.

6. Articles
Best for: In-depth analysis, thought leadership, or sharing comprehensive insights.
Tips: Write compelling headlines and use images to break up the text. Promote your articles through your network to increase visibility, similar to how you'd hype up the main event of your party.

P

POSTS

7. Newsletters
Best for: Building a loyal audience, sharing regular insights, and fostering deeper connections.
Tips: Craft engaging and informative content that resonates with your audience, similar to how you'd curate the perfect playlist for your party. Use eye-catching visuals and a consistent format to keep readers interested. Promote your newsletters through your network to increase visibility, just like you'd hype up a special event at your party to ensure everyone knows it's happening. Regularly engaging with your subscribers will help create a sense of community, making them eager to return for your next edition.

The Anatomy of a Perfect LinkedIn® Post

Headline: Start with a compelling headline that grabs attention, much like the exciting announcement of a surprise guest at your party.

Introduction: Write a strong opening sentence that hooks the reader. This should provide a glimpse of what the post is about, similar to setting the tone for the evening.

Body: Keep It Focused: Stick to one main idea or theme per post, just like a party that has a clear theme.

Structure: Use short paragraphs, bullet points, and whitespace to make the content easy to read, akin to creating space on the dance floor for everyone to move.

Visual Elements: Images/Videos: Use relevant and high-quality visuals to complement your text. This is like the dazzling lights that enhance the party atmosphere.

Emojis: Use sparingly to add personality and break up the text but keep it professional; think of them as fun party props that add flair without overwhelming the scene.

Call to Action (CTA): End with a clear CTA, inviting your audience to comment, share, or engage further. This is like encouraging guests to hit the dance floor or join in on a group activity.

Hashtags and Mentions: Use 3-5 relevant hashtags to increase the reach of your post. Mention relevant people or companies to boost engagement, like inviting special guests to join the fun.

P

POSTS

<u>Timing and Frequency:</u> Post 1-3 times per week to maintain a consistent presence, just like keeping the music flowing throughout the night. Engage with your audience within the first ninety minutes of posting to maximise visibility.

LinkedIn™ posts are your opportunity to create an engaging and dynamic atmosphere for your professional network, much like a lively disco party. By utilising the various types of posts effectively and following the perfect anatomy of a LinkedIn™ post, you can attract attention, foster connections, and showcase your expertise. So, get ready to light up the LinkedIn™ dance floor with your engaging posts and watch your professional presence thrive.

CHOICE POINTS

If you want to learn more about articles, turn to page 12.
To explore more about thought leadership, turn to page 182.
To delve into curated content, go to page 37.

TOP TIP

A study by OkDork, which analysed more than 3,000 LinkedIn® posts, found that 'how-to' and list posts performed best, especially those with titles that had 40-49 characters.

P

51. PRIVACY SETTINGS

Just as you would control the guest list and access at your exclusive disco party, managing your privacy settings on LinkedIn™ is essential for safeguarding your personal information and ensuring a secure online presence. LinkedIn™ offers a range of privacy settings that allow you to control what information is visible to others, how your data is used, and who can contact you.

Why Are Privacy Settings Important?

Control Over Personal Information
Privacy settings allow you to decide what information you want to share and with whom. This is like deciding who gets an invite to your party and who stays outside.

Enhanced Security
By managing your privacy settings, you can protect your account from unauthorised access and potential data breaches; it's like having bouncers at your party to ensure only invited guests enter.

Professional Image Management
Controlling who sees your profile and activity helps you maintain a professional image. This is similar to curating the guest experience at your party to ensure everyone has a great time.

Key Privacy Settings on LinkedIn®

1. Account Preferences: Manage your basic profile information, networking settings, and subscriptions. This is like setting up the basic infrastructure for your party, such as the venue and guest list.

2. Sign In & Security: Manage settings to keep your account secure, including password and two-step verification; it's like having security checks at the entrance of your party to ensure only invited guests can enter.

3. Visibility: Control who can see your profile, network, and LinkedIn™ activity. This is akin to deciding who can see different areas of your party, such as VIP sections or the main dance floor.

Profile Viewing Options: Choose between showing your name and headline, private profile characteristics, or viewing in private mode.

P

PRIVACY SETTINGS

Who Can See Your Connections: Decide if your connections can see your other connections.

4. Data Privacy: Configure privacy and security settings related to how LinkedIn™ uses your data and other applications. This is like controlling how much personal information you share with party vendors and sponsors.

How LinkedIn Uses Your Data: Manage the ways your data is used on LinkedIn™.

Who Can Reach You: Manage invitations and messages to control who can contact you.

Messaging Experience: Customise your messaging settings, such as read receipts and typing indicators.

Turning off LinkedIn™ InMails is like finally getting rid of those uninvited party crashers who keep interrupting your fun. Without the distractions, you can truly enjoy the company of your guests and focus on meaningful conversations.

5 Quick & Easy Steps to Stop LinkedIn™ InMails.

1) Open LinkedIn™ and click on the photo of you in the top right-hand corner called 'Me'.
2) From the drop-down, select 'Settings and Privacy'.
3) On the left-hand menu, select 'Data Privacy'.
4) Under the 'Who can reach you' menu on the right > click on 'Messages'.
5) 'Allow others to send you InMail?' switch this to off.

Inmails are different from your normal inbox messages. They stay on.

5. Advertising Data: Control the information that LinkedIn™ uses to show you relevant ads by adjusting your account's ad settings. This is like deciding which sponsors can advertise at your party and how.

6. Notifications: Enable or disable the types of notifications you want to receive and how often you wish to receive them; it's like deciding how often you want to make announcements at your party.

P

PRIVACY SETTINGS

Best Practices for Privacy Settings:

Regularly Review Settings: Periodically check and update your privacy settings to ensure they align with your current preferences and needs.

Use Strong Passwords: Ensure your account is protected with a strong, unique password and enable two-step verification.

Be Selective with Connections: Only connect with people you know or trust to maintain a secure and professional network.

Limit Data Sharing: Adjust settings to limit how your data is used and shared by LinkedIn™ and third-party applications.

Monitor Profile Views: Use profile viewing options to control who can see when you've viewed their profile and vice versa.

Managing your privacy settings on LinkedIn™ is crucial for maintaining a secure and professional online presence. By understanding and utilising the various privacy options available, you can control what information is shared, protect your data, and ensure that your LinkedIn™ experience is as safe and enjoyable as a well-managed disco party. Take the time to review and adjust your privacy settings and keep your professional network secure and thriving.

CHOICE POINTS

If you want to learn more about guidelines, turn to page 62.
To explore more about notifications, turn to page 110.
If you want to explore more about reputation management, turn to page 146.

P

52. PROFILE PHOTO

Your profile photo on LinkedIn™ is like the entrance to your disco party; it's the first thing people see and can significantly influence their perception of you. A well-chosen profile photo not only enhances your professional image but also helps you connect with others in your network.

Why is Your Profile Photo Important?

First Impressions Matter
Your profile photo is often the first point of contact for potential partners, clients, or collaborators. A professional and approachable image creates a positive first impression, much like a warm welcome at your party.

Increased Engagement
Profiles with photos receive more views and connection requests than those without, just like having an inviting entrance at your disco that draws guests in.

Brand Representation
Your photo reflects your personal brand and professionalism. Just as you would choose an outfit that represents your style and the theme of your party, your LinkedIn™ photo should convey your professional identity.

Best Practices for Your LinkedIn® Profile Photo:

1. *Use a High-Quality Image:* Ensure your photo is clear, well-lit, and of high resolution. This is like having bright, vibrant lighting at your party that showcases the best moments.

2. *Dress Professionally:* Wear attire that reflects your industry standards. Just as you would dress appropriately for a themed party, your outfit should match the professional context of LinkedIn™.

3. *Choose a Neutral Background:* A simple, uncluttered background helps keep the focus on you. This is similar to having a clean dance floor that allows guests to enjoy the music without distractions.

4. *Smile and Be Approachable:* A friendly expression can make you seem more approachable. Just as a warm smile invites guests to join the fun, a welcoming expression in your photo encourages connections.

P

PROFILE PHOTO

5. Crop Your Photo Appropriately: Your face should be the focal point of the image, ideally filling about 60% of the frame. This is like ensuring the best part of your party is front and centre, drawing attention to the highlights.

6. Avoid Distracting Elements: Steer clear of busy patterns or accessories that might divert attention from your face. This is akin to avoiding overwhelming decorations that take away from the party atmosphere.

7. Update Regularly: Keep your photo current, especially if your appearance changes significantly. Just as you would refresh your party theme or decor, updating your photo keeps your profile relevant.

Your LinkedIn™ profile photo is a crucial element of your professional presence, acting as the inviting entrance to your digital networking space. By following best practices for your photo, you can create a strong first impression, enhance engagement, and effectively represent your personal brand. So, choose a photo that reflects your professionalism and personality, and get ready to make connections as vibrant and engaging as the best disco party in town.

CHOICE POINTS

If you want to learn more about visibility, turn to page 197.
To explore more about your personal profile, turn to page 121.
To find out more about having an 'all-star' profile, turn to page 8.

TOP TIP
Upload a high definition photo. 1080 x 1080 is the perfect size for a LinkedIn® profile photo. Don't forget that it will be in a circle!

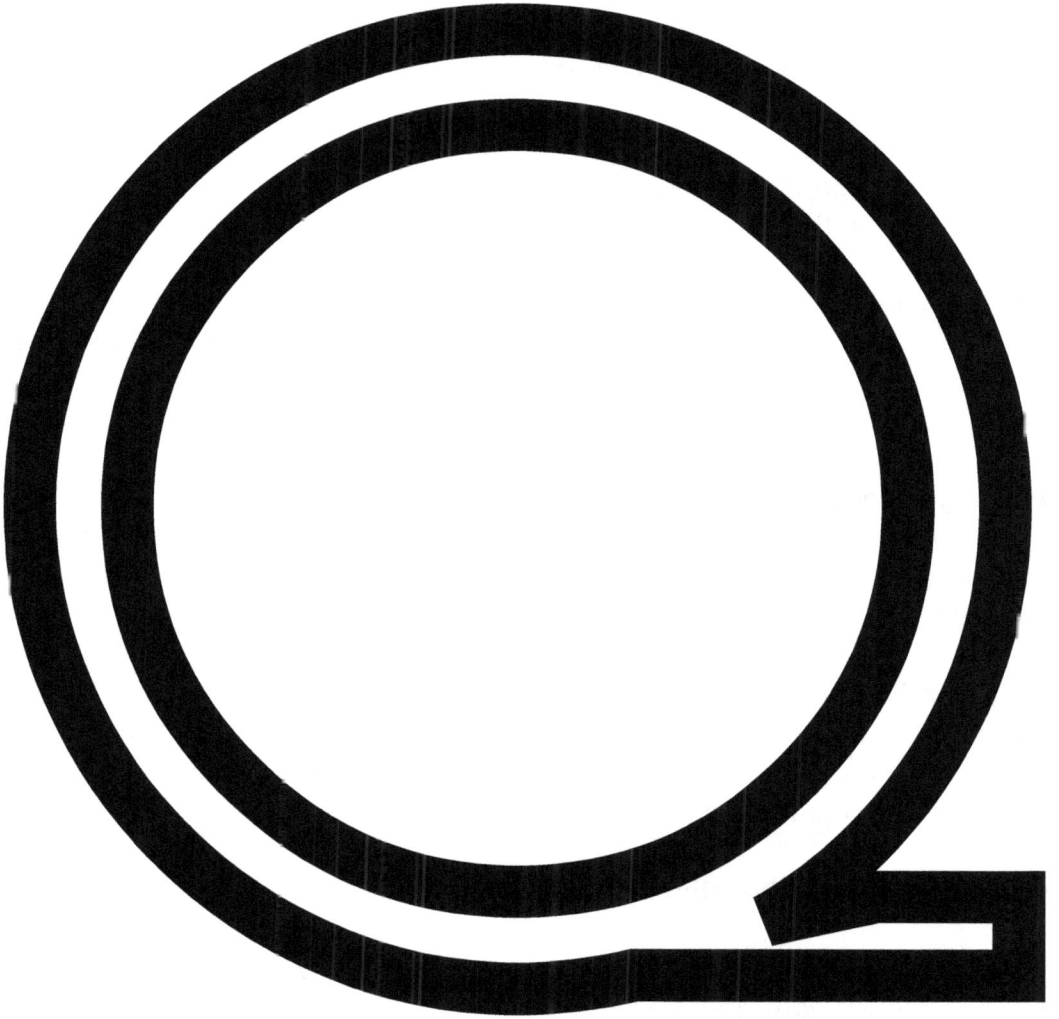

Q

53. QUESTIONS

Just as you might host a Q&A session or a trivia night at your disco party to engage guests and spark conversations, using questions on LinkedIn™ allows you to interact with your network, gather insights, and showcase your expertise.

Why Are Questions Important on LinkedIn®?

Engagement Boost
Questions encourage interaction from your network, increasing engagement on your posts. This is like getting party goers involved in fun activities, keeping the energy high.

Gathering Insights
Questions provide a quick and effective way to gather opinions and insights on specific topics. This feedback can inform your business decisions, much like asking guests for their favourite songs to play at your party.

Showcasing Expertise
By asking and answering questions related to your industry, you can position yourself as a thought leader. This is like leading a conversation about the latest trends in music at your disco.

Building Community
Questions foster a sense of community by inviting your connections to share their thoughts. This interaction can strengthen relationships, in the same way that shared activities at a party create bonds among guests.

How to Effectively Use Questions on LinkedIn®

1. *Choose Relevant Topics:* Select topics that resonate with your audience and are relevant to your industry. This ensures that the question is engaging and encourages participation.

2. *Keep It Simple:* Design questions that are straightforward and easy to understand. Complicated questions may deter participation, much like a confusing party game that leaves guests unsure of how to join in.

QUESTIONS

3. Encourage Participation: Promote your question through your network and enccurage connections to share their opinions. You can also follow up with a post discussing the responses to keep the conversation going.

4. Use Visuals: Incorporate images or graphics to make your question more visually appealing. This is similar to using vibrant decorations at your party to attract attention.

5. Engage with Responses: Respond to comments and engage with participants to deepen connections. This interaction is akin to mingling with guests at your party, making them feel valued and appreciated.

Best Practices for Asking Questions

Timing Matters: Post questions when your audience is most active to maximise participation. This is like choosing the right time to start a group activity at your party when energy levels are high.

Follow Up: After receiving responses, share insights or create a follow-up post to summarise the discussion. This keeps the conversation going, much like continuing a lively discussion from your party.

Mix It Up: Use a variety of question types, such as open-ended questions, polls, or multiple-choice questions. This variety keeps your audience engaged, similar to offering different types of activities at your party.

Be Authentic: Ask questions you genuinely want answers to. Your authenticity will shine through and encourage more meaningful responses.

Using questions on LinkedIn™ is a powerful tool for engaging your audience, gathering insights, and building community. By incorporating thoughtful questions into your content strategy, you can enhance your visibility, foster meaningful interactions, and position yourself as a thought leader in your industry. So, get ready to spark conversations and create engaging discussions that make your LinkedIn™ presence as dynamic and exciting as the best disco party in town.

Q

QUESTIONS

CHOICE POINTS

If you want to learn more about polls, turn to page 124.
To explore more about engagement, turn to page 48.
To delve into thought leadership, go to page 182.

TOP TIP

Be clear and concise, just like a well-planned party invitation. Your questions should be straightforward and easy to understand. Avoid jargon and keep your questions simple to encourage more responses.

R

54. RECOMMENDATIONS

Recommendations on LinkedIn™ are like the glowing reviews and testimonials you might receive after hosting a fantastic party. They serve as social proof of your skills, expertise, and professionalism, helping to establish your credibility and attract new opportunities.

Why Are Recommendations Important?

Credibility Boost

Recommendations enhance your professional image by providing third-party validation of your skills and accomplishments. Just as guests rave about your party to their friends, recommendations can influence potential employers or clients.

Trust Building

They help build trust with your network and potential connections. When others see positive feedback about you, they are more likely to engage and connect, much like how positive word-of-mouth can draw a crowd to your next event.

Networking Opportunities

Recommendations can lead to new connections and opportunities, as people are more likely to reach out to someone who is highly regarded by their peers.

Balanced Reciprocity

It's important to strive for a balance between the number of recommendations you give and receive. When you provide recommendations for others, it encourages them to return the favour. This reciprocity fosters stronger relationships and a sense of community, just like the way party guests who help each other have a better time are likely to return for future events.

Best Practices for Requesting and Giving Recommendations

1. Be Specific: When asking for a recommendation, specify the skills or experiences you would like the person to highlight. This makes it easier for them to write a focused and impactful recommendation.

2. Reciprocate: Make it a habit to give recommendations to others in your network. This not only strengthens your relationships but also encourages others to reciprocate, creating a balanced exchange.

R

RECOMMENDATIONS

3. Follow Up: After receiving a recommendation, thank the person and consider returning the favour. This is like sending thank you notes to guests who brought gifts to your party.

4. Keep It Professional: Ensure that your recommendations reflect your professional relationships and experiences, maintaining a level of professionalism that aligns with your brand.

Template for Requesting Recommendations:

To make it easier for someone to leave you a recommendation, consider providing them with a template of questions. Here's a simple template as a starting point:

Hi [Name],

I hope you're doing well. I'm currently looking to enhance my LinkedIn™ profile and would greatly appreciate it if you could provide me with a recommendation. Your feedback would mean a lot to me, especially considering our work together on [specific project or context].

To make it easier for you, here are a few questions you might consider addressing in your recommendation:

1. What was your overall impression of my work on [specific project or task]?
2. How did I contribute to the success of our team or project?
3. What specific skills or strengths did you notice during our collaboration?
4. How would you describe my work ethic and professionalism?
5. Would you recommend me for future opportunities? If so, why?

Thank you so much for considering this. If you need any further details or context, please feel free to reach out. I'm happy to reciprocate and provide a recommendation for you as well.

Best wishes,
[Your Name]

R

RECOMMENDATIONS

Recommendations on LinkedIn™ are a vital part of building your professional brand and establishing credibility. By actively seeking and giving recommendations, you create a balanced network of support and trust. Use the provided template to make it easier for others to leave you a recommendation and remember to reciprocate the kindness. With strong recommendations, you can enhance your LinkedIn™ presence and attract new opportunities, just like the rave reviews that keep guests coming back to your disco parties.

CHOICE POINTS

If you want to learn more about endorsements, turn to page 45.
To explore more about kudos, turn to page 85.
To delve into testimonials, go to page 180.

TOP TIP

When seeking recommendations on LinkedIn®, remember the importance of reciprocity.
Just like at a well-hosted party where everyone brings something to share, giving recommendations to others often encourages them to return the favour.

R

55. REFERRALS

Referrals on LinkedIn™ can be a powerful tool to expand your network, attract new clients, and foster partnerships. Just as a well-connected party host introduces guests to valuable contacts, leveraging referrals can significantly enhance your business relationships and opportunities, creating a vibrant atmosphere for growth.

Why Are Referrals Important?

Increased Credibility
Referrals provide third-party validation of your business' services and expertise. When someone vouches for your business, it adds credibility, much like having a well-respected guest at your disco party who can rave about the quality of the event.

Access to New Markets
Referrals can help you tap into new markets and industries, in the same way that exclusive invites can give certain guests access to special areas of your party, opening doors to exciting opportunities.

Faster Business Development
Potential clients and partners are more likely to consider businesses that come recommended by trusted connections. This can speed up the business development process, in the same way that a trusted friend can help you skip the queue at a popular venue, getting you right to the heart of the action.

Stronger Business Relationships
Requesting and giving referrals fosters deeper relationships within your network. This is like building camaraderie among party guests who share introductions and experiences, creating a lively and supportive community.

How to Effectively Request Referrals on LinkedIn®

1. Optimise Your Profile: Before reaching out for referrals, ensure your LinkedIn™ profile and company page are polished and professional. Highlight your business' services, achievements, and unique value propositions. A well-crafted profile serves as your online business card, making it easier for connections to endorse you, just like a well-decorated entrance sets the tone for your party.

R

REFERRALS

2. Identify the Right Connections: Look for business leaders, clients, or partners who can provide valuable referrals. This targeted approach is like inviting specific guests who can enhance the party atmosphere, ensuring you connect with the right people.

3. Craft a Personalised Message: When asking for a referral, personalise your message to show genuine interest. Avoid generic requests; instead, mention specific business opportunities or partnerships you're seeking. This is akin to making a personal connection with a guest before asking for an introduction, ensuring your request feels sincere and relevant.

4. Provide Context and Value: Explain your business' background and how it aligns with the referral's network or industry. Include any mutual connections or shared experiences to strengthen your request. This is like highlighting shared interests at your party to create rapport and foster connections.

5. Be Gracious and Respectful: Always thank your connections for considering your request regardless of their response. Maintaining a respectful tone helps build goodwill, just as a gracious host ensures all guests feel appreciated and valued.

Referrals on LinkedIn™ can significantly enhance your business development and networking efforts. By optimising your profile, identifying the right connections, and crafting personalised requests, you can effectively leverage referrals to unlock new opportunities. Just as a well-connected party host creates memorable experiences for guests, you can build valuable business relationships through referrals that lead to growth and success. Embrace the power of referrals and watch your business network flourish like the best disco party in town.

CHOICE POINTS

If you want to learn more about networking, turn to page 101.
To explore more about optimisation, turn to page 117.
To find out about finding leads, go to page 55.

R

56. REPUTATION MANAGEMENT

Reputation management on LinkedIn™ is like ensuring your disco is the talk of the town for all the right reasons; it's about curating and maintaining a professional image that reflects your expertise, credibility, and trustworthiness. Effective reputation management can lead to increased opportunities, stronger connections, and a more influential presence on the platform

Why is Reputation Management Important?

First Impressions

Your LinkedIn™ profile is often the first point of contact for potential partners, clients, or collaborators. A well-managed reputation ensures that this first impression is positive and professional, much like a well-organised party leaves guests impressed.

Credibility and Trust

A strong reputation builds credibility and trust within your network. Just as guests trust a well-known party host to deliver a great experience, your connections will trust you to deliver professional excellence.

Opportunities and Growth

A positive reputation can lead to new job offers, partnerships, and business opportunities. It's similar to how a successful party can lead to more invitations and collaborations.

Key Strategies for Reputation Management on LinkedIn®

1. Optimise Your Profile
Professional Photo: Use a high-quality, professional headshot.

Compelling Headline: Craft a headline that highlights your expertise and value proposition.

Engaging Summary: Write a summary that tells your professional story and showcases your skills and achievements.

Detailed Experience: Provide comprehensive information about your work history, focusing on accomplishments.

R

REPUTATION MANAGEMENT

2. Share Valuable Content

Regularly post content that showcases your expertise and thought leadership. This could include articles, industry insights, and updates on your professional activities. Use a mix of text, images, and videos to keep your content engaging.

3. Engage with Your Network

Actively participate in discussions, comment on posts, and share insights. This interaction helps build relationships and enhances your visibility. Join and contribute to LinkedIn™ groups related to your industry.

4. Collect and Give Recommendations

Recommendations serve as social proof of your skills and professionalism. Aim to have a balance between the number of recommendations you give and receive. This reciprocity fosters stronger relationships and a sense of community. When requesting a recommendation, provide a template or specific questions to make it easier for the person to write a meaningful endorsement.

5. Monitor and Respond to Feedback

Regularly check your LinkedIn™ notifications and messages. Respond promptly to comments and messages to show that you are engaged and approachable. Address any negative feedback professionally and constructively. This is like handling a guest complaint at your party with grace and efficiency.

6. Maintain Professionalism

Ensure that all interactions on LinkedIn™ reflect your professional image. Avoid controversial topics and maintain a respectful tone in all communications. Regularly update your profile to reflect your latest achievements and skills.

R

REPUTATION MANAGEMENT

Reputation management or LinkedIn™ is essential for building and maintaining a professional image that attracts opportunities and fosters trust. By optimising your profile, sharing valuable content engaging with your network, and balancing recommendations, you can enhance your reputation and ensure your LinkedIn™ presence is as impressive and memorable as the best disco party in town. So, take charge of your professional image and watch your network and opportunities grow.

CHOICE POINTS

If you want to learn more about optimisation, turn to page 117.
To explore more about content strategy, turn to page 34.
To find out more about thought leadership, go to page 182.

TOP TIP

If a misunderstanding or negative comment arises, address it quickly and professionally; it's like tactfully handling a party mishap before it becomes the talk of the town.

R

57. RESEARCH

Just as a savvy disco party host researches the latest music trends and guest preferences to create an unforgettable experience, conducting research on LinkedIn™ can provide valuable insights to fuel your business growth and networking strategies.

Why is LinkedIn® Research Important?

Market Intelligence
LinkedIn™ research helps you stay informed about industry trends, competitor activities, and potential opportunities; it's like keeping your finger on the pulse of the disco scene to ensure your party stays relevant and exciting.

Lead Generation
By researching potential clients or partners, you can tailor your approach and increase your chances of success. This is like identifying the VIP guests who can elevate your party's status.

Talent Acquisition
For businesses looking to hire, LinkedIn™ research can help identify potential candidates and understand the talent landscape; it's like scouting for the best DJs to keep your party's energy high.

Competitive Analysis
Researching competitors can provide insights into their strategies and positioning. This is similar to checking out other popular parties to see what makes them successful.

How to Conduct Effective Research on LinkedIn®

1. Utilise Advanced Search
Use LinkedIn™'s advanced search features to find specific individuals, companies, or job titles. This is like having a VIP list that helps you identify key guests at your party. Filter results by location, industry, and other relevant criteria to narrow down your search.

2. Leverage Company Pages:
Follow and analyse company pages to gain insights into their recent activities, job postings, and employee growth; it's like keeping an eye on other party venues to understand their offerings and popularity.

R

RESEARCH

3. Join and Monitor Groups
Participate in relevant LinkedIn™ groups to stay updated on industry discussions and trends. This is like joining exclusive clubs to stay in touch with the latest party themes and music.

4. Use LinkedIn™ Sales Navigator
For more advanced research, consider using LinkedIn™ Sales Navigator. This tool provides deeper insights and more powerful search capabilities, much like having a team of expert party planners at your disposal.

5. Analyse Content Engagement
Pay attention to the types of content that receive high engagement in your industry. This can inform your own content strategy, just as observing popular dance moves can help you plan your party's playlist.

6. Set Up the Notification Bell
Create alerts for specific companies, topics, or keywords to stay informed about relevant updates; it's like having scouts who keep you updated on the latest party trends and competitor activities.

Best Practices for LinkedIn® Research

Be Ethical: Respect privacy settings and use the information you gather responsibly. Just as you wouldn't spy on other parties, maintain professional boundaries in your research.

Stay Organised: Keep track of your findings in a systematic way. This could be like maintaining a party planning notebook with all your research and ideas.

Combine with Other Sources: While LinkedIn™ is a valuable resource, complement your research with other sources for a comprehensive view. This is like considering various aspects of party planning, from music to décor to catering.

Regularly Update Your Research: The business landscape is constantly changing. Regularly refresh your research to stay current, just as you would update your party playlist to include the latest hits.

R

RESEARCH

Conducting thorough research on LinkedIn™ can provide valuable insights to inform your business strategies, from lead generation to competitor analysis. By leveraging the platform's various features and following best practices, you can uncover information that gives you a competitive edge. Remember, just as a great disco party requires careful planning and awareness of trends, effective LinkedIn™ research can help you create a dynamic and successful business presence. So, put on your research hat, and get ready to discover insights that will make your business shine like a disco ball.

CHOICE POINTS

If you want to learn more about lead generation, turn to page 89.
To explore more about competitor analysis, turn to page 28.
To delve deeper into your target audience, go to page 177.

TOP TIP

Keep an eye on trending hashtags related to your research. This is similar to noticing which topics are generating the most buzz at your party, helping you stay informed about current trends and discussions.

S

58. SALES NAVIGATOR™

LinkedIn™ Sales Navigator™ is a premium tool designed to help business leaders and sales professionals leverage LinkedIn™'s extensive network to enhance their sales strategies, generate leads, and build valuable relationships. Much like having a VIP guest list for your disco party, Sales Navigator™ allows you to identify and engage with key prospects, ensuring your efforts are targeted and effective.

Why is Sales Navigator™ Important?

Advanced Search Capabilities
Sales Navigator™ offers advanced search filters to find the right prospects based on criteria such as job title, industry, location, and company size. This is like having a detailed guest list that helps you invite the most influential people to your party.

Lead Recommendations
Sales Navigator™ provides personalised lead recommendations, helping you discover potential clients you might not have considered; it's like having a party planner suggest VIP guests who can elevate your event.

InMail Messaging
Sales Navigator™ allows you to send direct messages to prospects outside your network, increasing your outreach capabilities. This is similar to sending exclusive invites to potential guests who aren't yet in your social circle.

Real-Time Insights
Stay updated with real-time insights on your leads and accounts, including job changes and company news. This is like having a live newsfeed of your party, keeping you informed about important developments.

TeamLink
Leverage your team's network to identify the best paths to introductions and referrals. This is like coordinating with your co-hosts to ensure everyone is connected and engaged.

S

SALES NAVIGATOR™

How to Use Sales Navigator™ Effectively

1. Optimise Your Profile
Ensure your LinkedIn™ profile is polished and professional. Highlight your business' services, achievements, and unique value propositions. A well-crafted profile serves as your online business card, making it easier for connections to endorse you.

2. Define Your Ideal Prospect
Clearly identify your target audience based on industry, job title, location, and other relevant factors. This is like knowing exactly who you want to invite to your party to create the best atmosphere.

3. Utilise Advanced Search Filters
Use Sales Navigator™'s advanced search features to find and segment potential leads. Filter by location, industry, current company, past company, and more. This helps you focus your efforts on the most promising prospects.

4. Engage with Prospects
Use InMail to reach out to potential clients with personalised messages. Reference common connections, shared interests, or their recent activities to make your outreach more relevant and engaging.

5. Monitor Lead Activity
Keep track of your leads' activities and updates to identify the best times to reach out. This is like monitoring your party guests to ensure everyone is having a good time and engaging with each other.

Best Practices for Sales Navigator™

Personalise Your Outreach: Customise your messages to make them relevant and engaging. Avoid generic pitches, and instead, show genuine interest in your prospects' needs and challenges.

Engage with Content: Share and comment on relevant content to increase your visibility and establish thought leadership. This is like playing the right music at your party to keep guests entertained and engaged.

154

S

SALES NAVIGATOR™

<u>Track Your Performance:</u> Use Sales Navigator™'s analytics tools to monitor your outreach efforts and adjust your strategy as needed. This is like keeping an eye on your party's vibe and adjusting to ensure everyone is having a great time.

<u>Stay Consistent:</u> Regularly update your lead lists and engage with your network to maintain momentum. Consistency is key to building strong relationships and achieving long-term success.

LinkedIn Premium and LinkedIn Sales Navigator™ are two different subscription offerings from LinkedIn™, each designed for specific purposes:

LinkedIn Premium is a more general-purpose subscription aimed at individual professionals; it's like having VIP access to a networking party, offering enhanced features for job seekers, professionals, and those looking to expand their network.

Sales Navigator™ is a specialised tool designed for sales professionals and teams; it's more like having a dedicated concierge at the networking party, helping you identify and connect with potential leads.

The main difference is that Sales Navigator™ is tailored specifically for sales professionals and teams looking to generate leads and manage customer relationships, while LinkedIn Premium offers a broader set of features for general professional networking and career development

Sales Navigator™ is a powerful tool for business leaders looking to enhance their sales strategies and build valuable relationships. By leveraging its advanced features and following best practices, you can effectively identify and engage with key prospects, much like curating a VIP guest list for your disco party. Embrace the power of Sales Navigator™ to unlock new opportunities and drive business growth, ensuring your professional presence is as dynamic and successful as the best party in town.

CHOICE POINTS

If you want to learn more about your social selling index, turn to page 166.
To explore more about strategy, turn to page 169.
To delve deeper into your lead generation, go to page 89.

S

59. SERVICES PAGE

Picture your LinkedIn™ profile as a bustling networking party, where professionals mingle and exchange ideas. Your Services Page is like setting up a special area at the party, showcasing your unique offerings to all the guests. Here's how to make the most of this feature:

Highlight Your Expertise
Your Services Page is where you display your professional skills like a dazzling array of party tricks. List your services clearly and concisely, making it easy for potential clients to understand what you offer. This is like having a well-designed menu at your party, enticing guests to try your specialties.

Use Compelling Visuals
Add eye-catching images or graphics to your Services Page. This is like decorating your party with attractive banners and displays that draw people's attention and make them want to learn more about what you're offering.

Provide Clear Descriptions
Offer detailed descriptions of your services. Think of this as explaining your party games or activities to interested guests, ensuring they understand exactly what they're signing up for.

Showcase Testimonials
Include client testimonials on your Services Page; it's like having satisfied party-goers recommend your party to others, building trust and credibility.

Keep It Updated
Regularly update your Services Page with new offerings or improvements. This is similar to refreshing your party with new attractions to keep guests coming back for more.

Engage with Enquiries
Respond promptly to any inquiries about your services. This is like being an attentive host at your party, ready to answer questions and make guests feel welcome.

S

59. SERVICES PAGE

To create a LinkedIn™ Services Page, follow these steps:

1.Access the Services Feature:
Go to your LinkedIn™ profile.
Look for the 'Add profile section' button.
Click on it and select 'Add services'.

2.Set Up Your Services:
Choose your service categories from the options provided.
Add a description of your services (up to 500 characters).
List up to 10 specific services you offer.

3.Add Visual Elements:
Upload a background image that represents your services.
Consider using eye-catching graphics or photos that showcase your work.

4.Provide Details:
Include information about your work process.
Mention any specialisations or unique selling points.

5.Showcase Testimonials:
If you have client testimonials, add them to your Services Page; this helps build credibility and trust.

6.Set Your Preferences:
Choose whether you want to be contacted about your services via LinkedIn™ messaging.

7.Review and Publish:
Double-check all the information you've entered.
Once you're satisfied, publish your Services Page.

59. SERVICES PAGE

Advantages of Optimising Your Services Page

Increased Visibility: A well-crafted Services Page improves your visibility on LinkedIn™. This is like having the most popular area at the party, attracting more guests and potential clients.

Direct Client Connections: The Services Page allows potential clients to contact you directly; it's just like having a VIP queue at your party where interested guests can easily reach you.

Establishing Authority: By showcasing your services professionally, you establish yourself as an authority in your field. This is like being known as the go-to expert at the party for specific skills or knowledge.

A LinkedIn® Services page versus a LinkedIn® Company page

A LinkedIn™ Services page and a Company page serve different purposes on the platform. Here's how they differ and why you might need both:

LinkedIn™ Services Page

Key features:
1. Highlights your individual professional services.
2. Appears on your personal profile.
3. Allows potential clients to contact you directly.
4. Ideal for freelancers, consultants, and solopreneurs.

LinkedIn™ Company Page

A Company page is more like hosting a separate corporate event within the larger LinkedIn™ party; it represents an organisation rather than an individual.

Key features:
1. Represents a business entity.
2. Allows multiple employees to be associated with it.
3. Provides a platform for company updates, job postings, and broader business marketing.
4. Ideal for businesses of all sizes, from start-ups to large corporations.

S

SERVICES PAGE
Do You Need Both?

Whether you need both depends on your professional situation:

1. For Solopreneurs/Freelancers: You might only need a Services page, as it's directly tied to your personal brand and the services you offer individually.
2. For Business Owners: If you run a company, even a small one, having both can be beneficial. Your Services page can showcase your personal expertise, while the Company page represents your business as a whole.
3. For Business Leaders: If you work for a company, you don't need a Services page unless you offer freelance services on the side. However, you should be associated with your company's page.

Why Have Both?

Having both pages can be advantageous because:

1. It separates your personal brand from your business brand.
2. It allows you to target different audiences (individual clients vs. business partners).
3. It provides more comprehensive networking opportunities.
4. It gives you flexibility in how you present your professional offerings.

In essence, a Services page is your personal spotlight at the LinkedIn™ party, while a Company page is like hosting a separate corporate event. Depending on your professional goals and structure, utilising both can maximise your presence and opportunities on the platform.

A LinkedIn™ Services page draws in potential clients, showcases your expertise, and opens up new opportunities for business growth. By putting effort into this feature, you ensure that your professional offerings stand out in the bustling LinkedIn™ marketplace, making your profile the life of the networking party.

CHOICE POINTS

If you want to learn more about company pages, turn to page 26.
To explore more about strategy, turn to page 169.
To delve deeper into your lead generation, go to page 89.

S

60. SKILLS SECTION

The Skills section on LinkedIn™ is like the playlist at your disco party; it highlights what you bring to the table and helps set the tone for your professional presence. This section allows you to showcase your abilities, making it easier for potential employers, clients, and connections to understand your expertise and value.

Why is the Skills Section Important?

Demonstrates Expertise

Listing your skills provides a clear picture of your professional capabilities. Just as a well-curated playlist gets guests excited about the music to come, a strong skills section showcases what you can offer.

Increases Profile Visibility

Profiles with skills listed are more likely to appear in search results when recruiters or potential clients are looking for specific expertise. This is like having the hottest tracks at your party that draw in the crowd.

Endorsements from Connections

The Skills section allows your connections to endorse your skills, adding credibility to your profile. This is like having guests rave about your party, boosting your reputation and encouraging others to join in.

Guides Networking Opportunities

By clearly defining your skills, you make it easier for others to connect with you for collaborations, projects, or job opportunities; it's like signalling to party-goers what kind of fun they can expect and who they might want to dance with.

How to Optimise the Skills Section

1. Choose Relevant Skills

Select skills that are relevant to your current industry and goals. Focus on both hard skills (technical abilities) and soft skills (interpersonal qualities). This is similar to creating a playlist that balances upbeat dance tracks with slower songs for variety.

2. Focus Your Skills

LinkedIn™ allows you to list up to 50 skills, but you can focus on 10-15 key skills that truly represent your expertise. This keeps your profile concise and impactful, much like a well-edited playlist that keeps the energy flowing without overwhelming guests.

S

SKILLS SECTION

3. Prioritise Your Top Skills
Pin your most important skills to the top of the list. This ensures that viewers see your key strengths first, just like starting your party with the most popular songs to get everyone on the dance floor.

4. Seek Endorsements
Encourage your connections to endorse your skills. You can do this by reaching out to colleagues, clients, or peers and asking them to endorse specific skills. This is like asking friends to share their favourite moments from your party, enhancing your credibility.

5. Update Regularly
As you gain new skills or shift your career focus, update your Skills section accordingly. This is like refreshing your party playlist to include the latest hits and keep the vibe current.

Best Practices for the Skills Section

Be Specific: Instead of broad terms, use specific skills that reflect your expertise. For example, instead of just "Marketing," specify "Digital Marketing" or "Content Marketing."

Showcase Unique Skills: If you have niche skills that set you apart from others in your field, make sure to include them. This is similar to featuring a unique dance move that becomes the highlight of your party.

Engage with Your Network: Regularly engage with your connections by commenting on their posts and endorsing their skills. This not only strengthens your relationships but can encourage them to return the favour.

The Skills section on LinkedIn™ is a vital component of your professional profile, showcasing your expertise and enhancing your visibility. By carefully selecting and optimising your skills, you can create a compelling representation of what you offer, much like a well-curated set list that keeps your disco party lively and engaging. Embrace the opportunity to highlight your skills, and watch as your professional network grows and thrives, just like the energy at the best party in town.

S

SKILLS SECTION

CHOICE POINTS

If you want to learn more about keywords, turn to page 83.
To explore more about endorsements, turn to page 45.
To delve deeper into recommendations, go to page 141.

TOP TIP
As you gain new experiences and knowledge, update your skills to reflect your growth. This is like refreshing your party menu for each event, keeping it exciting and relevant to your guests.

S

61. SOCIAL LISTENING

Social listening is the practice of monitoring social media channels for mentions, conversations, and trends related to a brand, industry, or topic. In the context of LinkedIn™, social listening involves tracking discussions and interactions that can provide valuable insights into your audience's preferences, sentiments, and behaviours. Just as a DJ listens to the crowd to understand what music resonates and keeps the energy alive, business owners can use social listening to tune into their audience's needs and enhance their engagement strategies.

Why Social Listening Matters

Customer Insights
Social listening allows businesses to gain a deeper understanding of their customers' thoughts and opinions. By tracking conversations on LinkedIn™, you can identify pain points, preferences, and emerging trends. This information is crucial for tailoring your products and services to better meet customer needs, much like how a DJ curates their setlist based on the crowd's reactions.

Reputation Management
Monitoring mentions of your brand on LinkedIn™ helps you manage your online reputation. By responding promptly to negative feedback or comments, you can address issues before they escalate, building trust and credibility with your audience. This proactive approach is akin to a DJ addressing a technical issue swiftly to keep the party going smoothly.

Competitor Analysis
Social listening also enables you to keep an eye on your competitors. By observing their social media activities and the conversations surrounding them, you can identify opportunities for differentiation and improvement. This is like how a DJ studies other artists' sets to find ways to stand out and create a unique experience.

Identifying Opportunities
Engaging with conversations related to your industry can reveal new opportunities for collaboration, partnerships, or product development. By tuning into what your audience is discussing, you can discover areas where your expertise can add value, just as a DJ might spot a chance to collaborate with another artist to create a fresh sound.

S

SOCIAL LISTENING

Enhancing Engagement

By understanding the topics that resonate with your audience, you can create content that sparks interest and encourages interaction. This is like a DJ knowing when to drop a popular track to get the crowd dancing, ensuring that your audience remains engaged and invested in your brand.

How to Get Started with Social Listening on LinkedIn®

1. Define Your Goals: Before diving into social listening, clarify what you hope to achieve. Are you looking to improve customer satisfaction, identify new product opportunities, or track competitor activity? Setting clear objectives will help focus your efforts and ensure you gather relevant data.

2. Choose the Right Tools: There are several social media monitoring tools available that can help you track mentions and conversations on LinkedIn™. When selecting a tool, consider factors such as ease of use, features, and pricing.

3. Identify Relevant Keywords: Determine the keywords and phrases related to your brand, industry, and competitors that you want to monitor. This could include your brand name, product names, industry terms, and competitor names. By tracking these keywords, you can capture relevant conversations and identify opportunities for engagement.

4. Analyse the Data: Once you've gathered data through social listening, analyse it to identify patterns and trends. Look for common themes and sentiments that can inform your social media strategy and help you make data-driven decisions.

5. Engage and Respond: Actively engage with your audience based on the insights you gather. Respond to comments, participate in discussions, and address any concerns. This engagement shows your audience that you value their input and are committed to building a relationship.

S

SOCIAL LISTENING

Social listening is a vital tool for business owners looking to understand their audience, enhance engagement, and build a strong online presence on LinkedIn™. By monitoring conversations and interactions, you can gain valuable insights that inform your marketing strategies, product development, and customer service improvements. Just as a DJ listens to the crowd to create an unforgettable party experience, social listening allows you to tune into your audience's needs and preferences, ensuring that your brand remains relevant and engaging. Embrace the power of social listening and watch your LinkedIn™ presence flourish.

CHOICE POINTS

If you want to learn more about building your brand, turn to page 21.
To explore more about engagement, turn to page 46.
To delve deeper into keywords, go to page 83.

TOP TIP
Follow up with connections to keep the conversation going. This is similar to checking in with guests after the party to thank them for coming and see how they enjoyed it.

S

62. SOCIAL SELLING INDEX (SSI)

The Social Selling Index (SSI) on LinkedIn™ is like a scorecard for your networking prowess at the professional disco party. It measures how effective you are at establishing your professional brand, finding the right people, engaging with insights, and building relationships. Just as a great party host keeps track of guest satisfaction and engagement, your SSI helps you gauge and improve your social selling efforts.

Why is the Social Selling Index Important?

Performance Measurement
SSI provides a quantifiable way to measure your social selling activities; it's like having a DJ booth that shows you how many people are dancing to each song you play.

Competitive Insight
You can compare your SSI with others in your industry and network. This is like seeing how your party stacks up against others in town.

Improvement Guide
The SSI breakdown helps identify areas where you can improve your social-selling strategy; it's like getting feedback on which aspects of your party need more attention.

Correlation with Success
LinkedIn™ reports that social-selling leaders create more opportunities, are more likely to reach quota, and outsell peers who don't use social-selling techniques. This is similar to how popular party hosts tend to have more successful events and broader networks.

S

SOCIAL SELLING INDEX (SSI)

The Four Pillars of SSI

1. Establish Your Professional Brand
Complete your profile with the customer in mind. Share relevant content regularly; this is like creating an inviting atmosphere and playlist that reflects your party's unique style.

2. Find the Right People
Use efficient search and research tools to identify better prospects. This is similar to curating your guest list to ensure the right mix of people at your party.

3. Engage with Insights
Share relevant content and engage with your network; it's like keeping your party guests entertained with interesting conversations and activities.

4. Build Relationships
Strengthen your network by connecting and engaging with decision makers. This is just like introducing guests to each other and fostering connections at your party.

How to Improve Your SSI Score

Optimise Your Profile: Ensure your profile is complete and professional. Include a high-quality photo, compelling headline, and detailed summary. This is like making sure your party venue looks inviting and well-prepared.

Share Valuable Content: Regularly post updates, articles, and insights relevant to your industry; it's like keeping the music fresh and exciting at your party.

Engage with Your Network: Comment on, like, and share posts from your connections. This is like mingling with guests and encouraging interactions at your party.

Use Sales Navigator™: If available, leverage Sales Navigator™ to find and engage with prospects more effectively. It's like having a VIP list and special access areas at your party.

S

SOCIAL SELLING INDEX (SSI)

<u>Join and Participate in Groups:</u> Engage in relevant LinkedIn™ groups to expand your network and share insights. This is like hosting themed areas or activities at your party to cater to different interests.

<u>Connect Strategically:</u> Focus on building meaningful connections with decision makers and influencers in your industry; it's like ensuring you personally greet and connect with key guests at your party.

How to Find Your SSI Score
Go to: https://www.linkedin.com/sales/ssi

The Social Selling Index on LinkedIn™ is a valuable tool for measuring and improving your professional networking effectiveness. By focusing on the four pillars of SSI and implementing strategies to improve your score, you can enhance your social selling skills and potentially drive better business results. Remember, just as a great party host continually refines their event-planning skills, improving your SSI is an ongoing process that can lead to more successful professional relationships and opportunities. Keep refining your approach, and watch your professional party become the talk of the LinkedIn™ town.

CHOICE POINTS

If you want to learn more about optimisation, turn to page 117.
To explore more about networking, turn to page 101.
To delve deeper into your content strategy, go to page 34.

$$\mathcal{S}$$

63. STRATEGY

A skilled party host plans every aspect of their event to ensure maximum enjoyment and engagement; a well-crafted LinkedIn™ strategy can help you achieve your professional goals and make meaningful connections. Let's explore how to create an effective LinkedIn™ strategy that will have your professional network dancing to your tune.

Key Components of an Effective LinkedIn® Strategy

Define Your Goals
Clearly outline what you want to achieve on LinkedIn™, whether it's generating leads, building brand awareness, or finding new business opportunities. This is like setting the theme for your party; it guides all your other decisions.

Optimise Your Profile
Ensure your profile is complete, professional, and engaging. This is the same as creating an inviting entrance to your party that makes people want to come in and learn more.

Content Strategy
Regularly share valuable content that resonates with your target audience. Mix different types of posts (text, images, videos) to keep things interesting, much like varying the music and activities at your party to keep guests engaged.

Engage with Your Network
Actively comment on, like, and share others' posts. This reciprocal engagement is like mingling with guests at your party, fostering connections and keeping the energy high.

Leverage Groups
Join and participate in relevant LinkedIn™ groups to expand your network and showcase your expertise. Just like hosting themed areas at your party where like-minded guests can connect.

Utilise LinkedIn® Features
Make use of new features to increase engagement. These are like special activities or performances that add excitement to your party.

S

STRATEGY

Implement a Referral Strategy

Develop a systematic approach to requesting and giving referrals. This is like encouraging guests to bring friends to your party, expanding your network organically.

Implementing Your LinkedIn® Strategy

1. Consistent Branding

Ensure your LinkedIn™ presence aligns with your overall brand identity. This consistency is like maintaining a cohesive theme throughout your party.

2. Schedule Regular Activity

Plan your content and engagement activities in advance. Aim to post 1-3 times per week and engage daily. This consistent presence keeps your network engaged, much like keeping the music playing throughout your party.

3. Monitor and Analyse

Regularly review your LinkedIn™ analytics to understand what's working and adjust your strategy accordingly, just like keeping an eye on which songs get people dancing and adjusting your playlist.

4. Personalise Your Approach

Tailor your connection requests and messages to each individual. Personalisation makes people feel valued, just as a good host makes each guest feel special at their party

5. Leverage Sales Navigator™

For more advanced strategies, especially in B2B sales, consider using LinkedIn™ Sales Navigator™. This tool can help you find and engage with the right prospects more effectively, like having a VIP list that ensures you're connecting with the most valuable guests.

S

STRATEGY

Top Tips for Your LinkedIn® Strategy

Curate Your Guest List (Strategic Connections)
Just as you wouldn't invite everyone in town to your exclusive disco, be selective with your LinkedIn™ connections; focus on quality over quantity. Connect with professionals who align with your business goals or industry; it's like ensuring your party has the right mix of people to create a vibrant atmosphere.

Perfect Your Party Outfit (Optimise Your Profile)
Your LinkedIn™ profile is your disco attire. Make sure it's polished and eye-catching. Use a professional photo, craft a compelling headline, and write an engaging 'About' section; it's like wearing your best disco outfit to make a lasting impression.

Be the Life of the Party (Engage Regularly)
Don't be a wallflower at your own party. Regularly share insightful posts, comment on others' content, and participate in relevant discussions; it's like being an energetic host, keeping the party lively and engaging.

Mix Your Tunes (Varied Content)
Just as a great DJ mixes different music styles, vary your content. Share industry news, personal insights, and professional achievements. This keeps your 'dance floor' (your feed) interesting and engaging for your connections.

Create VIP Areas (LinkedIn™ Groups)
Join or create LinkedIn™ groups related to your industry. This is like setting up VIP lounges at your disco where professionals with similar interests can gather and have more focused discussions.

Showcase Your Dance Moves (Skills and Endorsements)
Highlight your skills and seek endorsements from colleagues; it's like showing off your best dance moves, demonstrating what you're great at to impress other party-goers.

Plan Special Events (LinkedIn™ Articles)
Occasionally publish long-form articles on LinkedIn™. This is like hosting special themed nights at your disco, giving you a chance to showcase your expertise in depth.

S

STRATEGY

Keep the Party Going (Consistent Activity)
Maintain a consistent presence on LinkedIn™; it's like ensuring your disco is open regularly, so people know they can always drop by for some professional networking.

Mind Your Party Manners (Professional Etiquette)
Always maintain professional decorum in your interactions; it's like following disco etiquette - be respectful, avoid controversial topics, and maintain a positive atmosphere.

Exclusive Invitations (Personalised Outreach)
When reaching out to new connections, send personalised invitations; it's like handing out VIP passes with a personal touch, making each new connection feel valued.

A well-executed LinkedIn™ strategy can transform your professional presence from a quiet gathering to the hottest networking party in town. By defining clear goals, consistently engaging with your network, sharing valuable content, and leveraging LinkedIn™'s features, you can create a vibrant and successful professional presence. Remember, just as a great party evolves with the energy of its guests, your LinkedIn™ strategy should be flexible and responsive to your network's engagement.

CHOICE POINTS

If you want to learn more about goals, turn to page 208.
To explore more about engagement, turn to page 46.
To delve deeper into your content strategy, go to page 34.

T

T

64. TAGS AND MENTIONS

Tags and mentions are essential features on LinkedIn™ that facilitate engagement and connection within the professional network. Understanding how to use them effectively can enhance your visibility and foster relationships, but business owners should also exercise caution. Here's an overview of what tags and mentions are, their benefits, and why careful use is crucial.

What Are Tags and Mentions?

Tags

When you tag someone on LinkedIn, you use the '@' symbol followed by their name in a post, comment, or article. This action notifies the individual that they have been mentioned, creating a clickable link to their profile. For example, if you write a post about a collaboration, tagging the person involved will draw their attention and potentially their network's attention as well. Think of tagging as shining a spotlight on a guest at your disco party, highlighting their presence and encouraging others to engage.

Mentions

Mentions refer to the act of referencing another LinkedIn™ member, which can include tagging or simply mentioning their name without the '@' symbol. While tagged mentions are more formal and noticeable, untagged mentions can also be effective in conversations. This is like casually calling out to a friend across the dance floor, ensuring they feel included in the fun.

Hashtags

Whilst not the same as mentions, hashtags can be included in your posts to categorise content and increase its discoverability. Clicking on a hashtag leads to a page that aggregates all posts using that tag, in the same way that a disco ball reflects light around the room, drawing attention to various areas of the dance floor.

T

TAGS AND MENTIONS

Why Should Business Owners and Leaders Be Careful Using Tags and Mentions?

1. Professional Reputation: Misusing tags or mentions can lead to misunderstandings or negative perceptions. For instance, tagging someone in a post that they may not agree with can damage relationships. Just as a DJ must carefully select tracks to maintain a positive atmosphere, business owners and leaders should be mindful of how they mention others to protect their professional reputation. A poorly chosen track can clear the dance floor, just as a misplaced tag can alienate connections.

2. Notification Overload: Frequent or irrelevant tagging can annoy recipients. If you tag someone in every post, it may lead to notifications being ignored or even result in the person unfollowing or disconnecting. This is much like a DJ overplaying a popular song to the point where it loses its appeal, causing guests to lose interest in the party. Too many notifications can feel like a strobe light flashing incessantly, distracting and overwhelming.

3. Visibility Settings: Not all mentions will be seen by the intended audience if the tagged member has adjusted their visibility settings. If someone has turned off notifications for mentions, they won't receive alerts when they are tagged. This can lead to missed opportunities for engagement, just like a party where guests are unaware of exciting activities happening around them because they're too far from the mirror ball's glow.

4. Context Matters: The context in which you tag or mention someone is crucial. If the content does not relate to the person being mentioned, it may come across as spammy or insincere. This is like a DJ playing a track that doesn't fit the mood of the party, which can disrupt the flow and alienate the audience. A well-timed song can energise the crowd, while a mismatched one can bring the vibe crashing down.

5. Brand Image: For businesses, every mention reflects on the brand. Careless tagging or mentioning can lead to a negative impression of the company. Just as a disco party's success relies on the DJ's ability to create a cohesive experience, a brand's image hinges on how it communicates and engages with its audience. A dazzling mirror ball can enhance the atmosphere, but if the music is off, even the best decorations won't save the night.

T

TAGS AND MENTIONS

Tags and mentions on LinkedIn™ are powerful tools for enhancing engagement and building connections. However, business owners and leaders must use them thoughtfully to maintain their professional reputation, avoid overwhelming recipients, and ensure that their brand image remains intact. By being strategic and considerate in your approach, you can leverage tags and mentions effectively, creating a vibrant and engaging presence on LinkedIn™, much like a well-curated disco party that leaves guests wanting more. Just as a mirror ball reflects light and creates a captivating atmosphere, thoughtful tagging and mentioning can illuminate your professional network and foster meaningful connections.

CHOICE POINTS
To learn more about your reputation management, turn to page 146.
To explore more about engagement, turn to page 46.
To delve deeper into hashtags, go to page 65.

TOP TIP
After tagging someone, be sure to engage with any comments or responses they provide. This is like making sure to dance with your friends after inviting them to join you, keeping the energy up and the conversation flowing.

T

65. TARGET AUDIENCE

Understanding and engaging your target audience on LinkedIn™ is crucial for building meaningful connections, generating leads, and achieving your professional goals. Just as a successful disco party requires inviting the right guests to create the perfect atmosphere, identifying and engaging your target audience ensures your LinkedIn™ efforts are effective and impactful.

Why is Identifying Your Target Audience Important?

Focused Efforts

Knowing your target audience allows you to tailor your content and engagement strategies to meet their specific needs and interests. This is like curating a playlist that resonates with your party guests, ensuring everyone has a great time.

Increased Engagement

Engaging with the right audience leads to higher interaction rates, as your content will be more relevant and valuable to them. This is similar to having the right mix of people at your party, creating a lively and engaging atmosphere.

Better ROI (Return On Investment)

Targeting the right audience helps you achieve better results from your LinkedIn™ activities, whether it's lead generation, brand awareness, or networking. This is like investing in the best DJ and decorations to ensure your party's success.

How to Identify Your Target Audience on LinkedIn®

1. Define Your Ideal Client Profile (ICP)
Identify the characteristics of your ideal clients, such as industry, job title, company size, and location. This is like knowing the type of guests you want at your party to create the desired vibe.

2. Use Advanced Search Filters
Leverage LinkedIn™'s advanced search features to find individuals and companies that match your ICP. Filter by criteria like industry, job title, and location to narrow down your search. This helps you focus your efforts on the most relevant prospects.

T

TARGET AUDIENCE

3. Analyse Your Current Network

Look at your existing connections to identify common traits among those who engage most with your content. This is like observing which guests are enjoying your party and why.

4. Join Relevant Groups

Participate in LinkedIn™ groups that are relevant to your industry and interests. This allows you to connect with like-minded professionals and potential clients; it's like joining themed areas at a party where guests with similar interests gather.

5. Monitor Competitors

Analyse the followers and engagement on your competitors' profiles to identify potential audience segments you may have overlooked, in the same way that you might check out other popular parties to see what makes them successful.

Engaging Your Target Audience on LinkedIn®

<u>Create Valuable Content:</u> Share content that addresses the needs and interests of your target audience. This could include industry insights, tips, and thought-leadership articles. Just as a great playlist keeps party guests entertained, valuable content keeps your audience engaged.

<u>Personalise Your Outreach:</u> When connecting with new prospects, personalise your messages to show genuine interest and relevance. This is like personally inviting guests to your party, making them feel valued and welcomed.

<u>Engage with Their Content:</u> Actively like, comment on, and share posts from your target audience. This reciprocal engagement builds relationships and increases your visibility; it's like mingling with guests at your party, fostering connections and conversations.

<u>Utilise LinkedIn™ Features:</u> Use features like the notification bell and polls to create interactive and engaging content. These features can help you reach a wider audience and encourage participation, much like special activities or performances at your party.

<u>Leverage LinkedIn™ Sales Navigator:</u> For more advanced targeting, use LinkedIn™ Sales Navigator to find and engage with prospects more effectively. This tool provides deeper insights and more powerful search capabilities, like having a VIP list for your party.

T

TARGET AUDIENCE

Best Practices for Engaging Your Target Audience

1. Consistency is Key: Regularly post and engage with your audience to maintain visibility and build relationships. Consistency keeps your audience engaged, much like a steady flow of great music keeps the party lively.

2. Use the Bell Notification: To stay updated on what your target audience is doing on LinkedIn™, activate the bell notification on their profiles. This feature acts like a spotlight at a disco, ensuring that you're always in the loop about their latest activities and insights. By doing so, you can engage with their updates and maintain meaningful connections, making sure your professional relationships shine brightly in the LinkedIn™ landscape.

3. Be Authentic: Authenticity resonates with people. Share your experiences and insights genuinely to build trust and rapport. This is akin to being a gracious and genuine host at your party.

4. Measure and Adjust: Use LinkedIn™ analytics to track the performance of your content and engagement efforts. Adjust your strategy based on what works best. This is like tweaking your party setup based on guest feedback to ensure everyone has a great time.

Identifying and engaging your target audience on LinkedIn™ is essential for building meaningful connections and achieving your professional goals. By defining your ideal client profile, using advanced search filters, creating valuable content, and leveraging LinkedIn™ features, you can effectively reach and engage the right people. Just as a successful disco party requires the right mix of guests and activities, a well-executed LinkedIn™ strategy ensures your professional presence is vibrant and impactful. Embrace these strategies and watch your LinkedIn™ network grow and thrive.

CHOICE POINTS

If you want to learn more about engagement, turn to page 46.
To explore more about your unique value proposition, turn to page 188.
To delve deeper into your connections, go to page 32.

T

66. TESTIMONIALS

Testimonials and recommendations on LinkedIn™ are both valuable forms of social proof that can enhance your professional profile, but they have some key differences. Let's explore how testimonials differ from recommendations.

Format: Testimonials are typically shorter quotes or statements that can be displayed in various sections of your profile or on your website; they're like having snippets of praise scattered throughout your disco venue.

Flexibility: You have more control over how and where testimonials are displayed. This allows you to strategically place them, much like positioning complimentary comments around your party space.

Source: Testimonials can come from a wider range of sources, including clients or customers who may not be LinkedIn™ connections, just like collecting positive feedback from party attendees, even if they're not regular guests.

Length: Testimonials are often shorter and more concise than recommendations; they're like quick, enthusiastic shouts of approval heard over the music at your disco.

Customisation: You can often edit or curate testimonials to highlight specific aspects of your work, much like choosing the most flattering comments to display about your party.

Key Differences:

1. *Platform Integration:* Recommendations are a native LinkedIn™ feature, while testimonials can be used across various platforms. Recommendations are like the official guest book at your party, while testimonials are like positive reviews shared on various social media platforms.

2. *Verification:* LinkedIn™ recommendations are verified as they're linked to user profiles, whereas testimonials may require additional verification. This is like having signed guest comments versus anonymous praise for your party.

3. *Depth:* Recommendations often provide more detailed accounts of professional relationships, while testimonials are typically more concise; it's the difference between a detailed review of your party and a quick 'Great party!' comment.

T

TESTIMONIALS

4. Placement: Recommendations have a fixed location on your profile, while testimonials can be strategically placed throughout your professional materials. This is like having a dedicated wall of fame at your party versus spreading positive quotes throughout the venue.

To maximise your LinkedIn™ presence, consider using both recommendations and testimonials. Encourage connections to write recommendations on your profile, and collect testimonials to use strategically in your summary, experience sections, or on your website. This comprehensive approach will help create a well-rounded and impressive professional image, much like a disco party that receives rave reviews both in the official guestbook and across various social platforms.

CHOICE POINTS

If you want to learn more about recommendations, turn to page 141.

To explore more about kudos, turn to page 85.

To delve deeper into your endorsements, go to page 45.

TOP TIP

If a client seems unsure about what to write, provide them with a few prompts or examples. This is like giving your friends a nudge to remember the best parts of the party, helping them articulate their thoughts more clearly.

T

67. THOUGHT LEADERSHIP

Thought leadership on LinkedIn™ is about positioning yourself as an expert and authority in your industry. Just as a charismatic DJ sets the tone for an unforgettable disco party, a thought leader shapes conversations and influences opinions within their professional network.

Why is Thought Leadership Important?

Builds Credibility
Thought leadership establishes your credibility and expertise in your field; it's like being the DJ who knows all the best tracks and keeps the dance floor packed.

Enhances Visibility
Sharing valuable insights and perspectives increases your visibility on LinkedIn™, attracting more followers and connections. This is similar to having a spotlight on you at the party, making you the centre of attention.

Fosters Trust
Consistently providing valuable content helps build trust with your audience. Just as guests trust a skilled DJ to keep the music flowing, your network will trust your insights and recommendations.

Generates Opportunities
Thought leadership can lead to new business opportunities, partnerships, and speaking engagements. It's like being invited to DJ at other high-profile events because of your reputation.

How to Establish Thought Leadership on LinkedIn®

1. Create High-Quality Content
Share articles, posts, and updates that provide valuable insights and address industry trends, just like curating a playlist that resonates with your audience and keeps them engaged.
Use a mix of content formats, including text posts, videos, and infographics, to cater to different preferences.

T

THOUGHT LEADERSHIP

2. Engage with Your Network
Actively participate in discussions by commenting on and sharing others' posts. This interaction helps you build relationships and increase your visibility, much like mingling with guests at your party.
Respond to comments on your posts to foster a sense of community and show that you value your audience's input.

3. Leverage LinkedIn™ Features
Publish long-form articles on LinkedIn™ to delve deeper into topics and showcase your knowledge.

4. Join and Contribute to Groups
Participate in LinkedIn™ groups related to your industry to share insights and engage with like-minded professionals, just like joining themed areas at your party where guests with similar interests gather.
Consider starting your own group to create a community around your thought leadership.

5. Collaborate with Other Thought Leaders
Partner with other experts in your field for joint webinars, articles, or projects. This collaboration can expand your reach and credibility, much like a DJ collaborating with other artists to create a memorable event.

6. Showcase Your Achievements
Highlight your accomplishments, awards, and recognitions on your LinkedIn™ profile. This is like displaying your DJ trophies and accolades at your party to impress guests.
Use the Featured section to showcase your best work, including articles, presentations, and videos.

CHOICE POINTS

If you want to learn more about content strategy, turn to page 34.
To explore more about engagement, turn to page 46.
To delve deeper into visibility, go to page 197.

T

68. TRENDING TOPICS

Trending topics on LinkedIn™ are crucial for professionals looking to engage with their network, share insights, and position themselves as thought leaders in their respective fields. Just as a successful disco party thrives on the latest hits and trends, staying updated on trending topics can enhance your professional presence and foster meaningful connections.

Why are Trending Topics Important?

Increased Engagement
Posting about trending topics can lead to higher engagement rates as your content resonates with current discussions. This is similar to playing the latest chart-toppers at your party, which keeps guests excited and dancing.

Establishing Thought Leadership
By sharing your insights on trending topics, you can position yourself as a thought leader in your industry. Just as a DJ curates the perfect playlist to showcase their expertise, your contributions can highlight your knowledge and perspective.

Networking Opportunities
Engaging with trending topics allows you to connect with like-minded professionals and expand your network, in the same way guests at a party bond over shared interests and popular music.

Staying Relevant
Keeping up with trends ensures that your content remains relevant and timely, much like adjusting your party theme to reflect current trends, ensuring guests feel engaged and connected.

How to Identify and Engage with Trending Topics on LinkedIn®

1. *Follow Industry Leaders:* Keep an eye on posts from industry leaders and influencers. Their insights often highlight emerging trends and discussions. This is like following the most popular DJs to see what tracks are making waves.

2. *Join Relevant Groups*: Participate in LinkedIn™ groups related to your industry to stay updated on the latest conversations and topics. In the same way that you might join an exclusive clubs where the latest trends are discussed.

T

TRENDING TOPICS

3. Utilise LinkedIn™'s Content Suggestions: LinkedIn™ provides content suggestions based on your interests and network. Use this feature to discover trending topics that align with your expertise, much like a DJ selecting tracks based on the crowd's preferences.

4. Engage with Hashtags: Search for and follow relevant hashtags to see what topics are currently trending; it's like tuning in to the hottest music charts to stay informed about popular songs.

5. Monitor LinkedIn™ News: Keep an eye on LinkedIn™'s news section for updates on industry trends and discussions, just as a DJ might check the latest music releases to ensure your party playlist is fresh and exciting.

Best Practices for Engaging with Trending Topics

<u>Share Your Insights:</u> When discussing trending topics, share your unique perspective and insights. This adds value to the conversation and positions you as an expert, much like a DJ who mixes their style with popular tracks.

<u>Use Engaging Formats:</u> Consider using videos, polls, or infographics to present your thoughts on trending topics. This variety keeps your content engaging, similar to the way a DJ mixes different genres to keep the dance floor lively.

<u>Encourage Discussion:</u> Ask open-ended questions related to trending topics to encourage engagement from your network, much like inviting guests to share their thoughts on the music, fostering a lively conversation.

<u>Stay Authentic:</u> While it's important to engage with trends, ensure your contributions align with your personal brand and values. Authenticity resonates with your audience, just as a DJ's genuine passion for music shines through in their sets.

T

TRENDING TOPICS

Engaging with trending topics on LinkedIn™ is essential for building your professional presence and fostering meaningful connections. By staying updated on industry trends, sharing your insights, and participating in discussions, you can position yourself as a thought leader and enhance your visibility. Just as a successful disco party thrives on the latest hits and trends, your LinkedIn™ strategy should reflect current conversations to keep your network engaged and growing. Embrace the power of trending topics, and watch your professional influence expand like the energy on the dance floor.

CHOICE POINTS

If you want to learn more about groups, turn to page 60.
To explore more about content strategy, turn to page 34.
To delve deeper into industry insights, go to page 74.

TOP TIP
Comment on and share posts related to trending topics from others in your network. This is like inviting others to join you on the dance floor, fostering connections and encouraging collaboration.

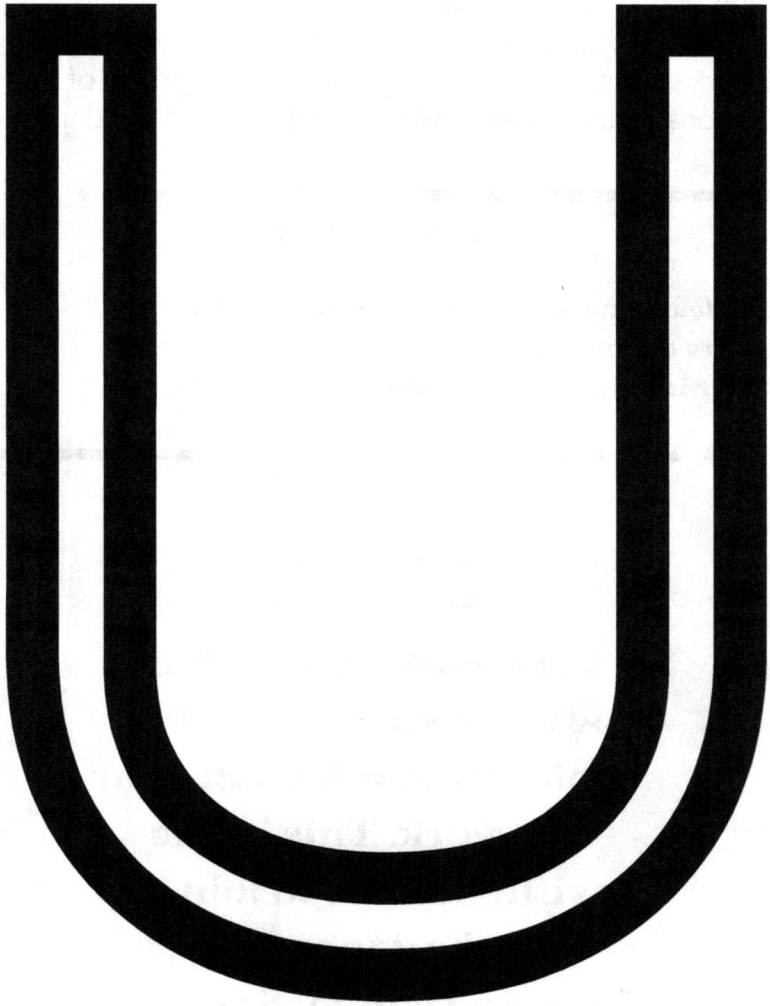

U

69. UNIQUE VALUE PROPOSITION

Crafting a Unique Value Proposition (UVP) for your LinkedIn™ profile is essential for standing out in your industry and attracting the right connections and opportunities. Your UVP is like the signature sound that makes your disco party unforgettable - it's what sets you apart from the crowd and makes people want to engage with you.

Here's how to create a compelling UVP for your LinkedIn® profile

Understand Your Audience
Identify your target audience on LinkedIn™, just as you'd consider your ideal party guests; research their needs, challenges, and goals to tailor your UVP effectively.

Define Your Unique Strengths
Pinpoint what makes you different from others in your field, just like identifying your unique DJ style that makes your parties stand out. Consider your skills, experiences, and achievements that are most relevant to your audience.

Focus on Benefits
Highlight how your unique qualities benefit your audience. This is like explaining why your party is the must-attend event of the season. Use clear, concise language to communicate these benefits.

Be Specific and Measurable
Include concrete examples or metrics that demonstrate your value, just like you might showcase your party's attendance numbers or rave reviews. Use numbers and specific achievements to make your UVP more impactful.

Keep It Concise
Your UVP should be brief and easy to understand, much like a catchy tagline for your disco party. Aim for a clear, memorable statement that can be quickly grasped.

Test and Refine
Get feedback on your UVP from colleagues or mentors, like asking for input on your party playlist. Be prepared to tweak and improve your UVP based on the responses you receive.

U

UNIQUE VALUE PROPOSITION

When crafting your UVP, consider using this formula:

'I help [target audience] achieve [desired outcome] through [your unique approach/skills].'

For example:
'I help small businesses increase their online visibility by 50% through innovative, data-driven digital marketing strategies.'

Remember, your UVP should be prominently displayed in your LinkedIn™ headline and summary section; it should also be reflected throughout your profile, including in your experience descriptions and skills section.

By creating a strong UVP, you'll make your LinkedIn™ profile as memorable and engaging as the hottest disco in town, attracting the right connections and opportunities to grow your professional network and career.

CHOICE POINTS

If you want to learn more about visibility, turn to page 197.
- **To explore more about your target audience, turn to page 177.**
- **To delve deeper into your headline, go to page 67.**

TOP TIP
Use straightforward language that resonates with your audience, just as you would choose catchy lyrics that everyone can sing along to.

U

70. URL CUSTOMISATION

Go from: https://www.linkedin.com/in/esther-partridge-97930a159/
to: https://www.linkedin.com/in/estherpartridge/

Customising your LinkedIn™ URL is a simple yet impactful step that can significantly enhance your professional image and online presence. Just as a well-crafted disco ball reflects light and draws attention at a party, a personalised LinkedIn™ URL can help you shine in the professional world.

Here's why you should consider making this change:

1. Easier to Find and Share

A custom LinkedIn™ URL makes your profile easier to locate and share. If you have a common name, a personalised URL can help differentiate you from others. This is particularly beneficial when potential clients or connections search for you on LinkedIn™ or Google. A clean, memorable URL simplifies the process of finding your profile, much like having a catchy name for your disco party that makes it easy for guests to remember and talk about.

2. Boosts Your Credibility

Having a customised URL signals that you are detail-oriented and serious about your professional brand. It shows that you've taken the time to present yourself well online, which can leave a positive impression on followers and potential connections. This attention to detail can set you apart from other businesses, the way a well-planned disco party impresses guests with its thoughtful décor and vibrant atmosphere.

3. Professional Branding

A personalised URL contributes to a cohesive professional brand. It allows you to include your name, profession, or a unique identifier that reflects your expertise. This consistency can enhance your overall online presence, making it easier for people to remember you and your brand. Just as a DJ develops a unique sound that becomes their signature, a customised URL helps establish your identity in the professional world, ensuring you stand out like a dazzling disco ball in a dimly lit room.

U

URL CUSTOMISATION

4. Use in Professional Materials

Including your LinkedIn™ URL on your website, business cards, and email signature is essential for making it easy for others to connect with you. A messy URL filled with random characters is less likely to be shared or remembered. A neat, customised URL looks professional and is more likely to encourage others to visit your profile. Think of it as the perfect invitation to your disco party; if it's eye-catching and easy to read, more people will want to join in on the fun.

Here are some examples of customised public profile URLs to inspire you:

Your Name: If your name is distinctive or if you have a personal brand, using your name in the URL is an excellent choice.
For example, linkedin.com/in/estherpartridge/

Your Profession: If you want to emphasise your profession or area of expertise, consider including it in the URL.
For example, linkedin.com/in/estherpartridgecoach/

Your Company Name: If you work for a prominent company, incorporating its name into your URL can help you stand out.
For example, linkedin.com/in/estherpartridgeonlinemediaworks/

Your Location: If you operate in a specific area or wish to attract local clients, including your location in the URL can be beneficial.
For example, linkedin.com/in/estherpartridgeworcester/

A Memorable Phrase: To create a unique and memorable URL, consider using a catchy phrase that reflects your brand or personality.
For example, linkedin.com/in/estherpartridgelinkedinqueen/

How to Customise your LinkedIn® URL

To customise your LinkedIn™ URL, follow these steps:

1. *Go to Your Profile:* Log in to LinkedIn™ and navigate to your profile by clicking on your profile picture or the 'Me' icon at the top of the homepage.
2. *Edit Public Profile & URL:* On your profile page, look for the option that says 'Edit public profile & URL' on the right sidebar. Click on it.

U

URL CUSTOMISATION

3. Customise Your URL: In the top right corner of the new page, you'll see a section labelled 'Edit your custom URL.' Click on the pencil icon next to your current URL.

4. Enter Your Desired URL: Type in your desired custom URL. This should be simple, professional, and ideally include your name or a variation that represents your personal brand.

5. Save Changes: After entering your new URL, click 'Save' to apply the changes.

Customising your LinkedIn™ URL is a small but significant step that can enhance your professional image, improve your visibility, and make it easier for others to connect with you. By taking the time to create a memorable and professional URL, you can set yourself apart in the competitive world and strengthen your online presence. Just as a disco ball reflects light and creates a captivating atmosphere, a personalised URL can help you shine brightly in your professional network. Embrace this simple change and watch as it positively impacts your networking and career opportunities.

DID YOU KNOW?

Around 65 % of professionals now recognise that an online impression can be just as significant as one made in person.

CHOICE POINTS

If you want to learn more about your personal profile, turn to page 121.

To explore more about visibility, turn to page 197.

To delve deeper into keywords, go to page 83.

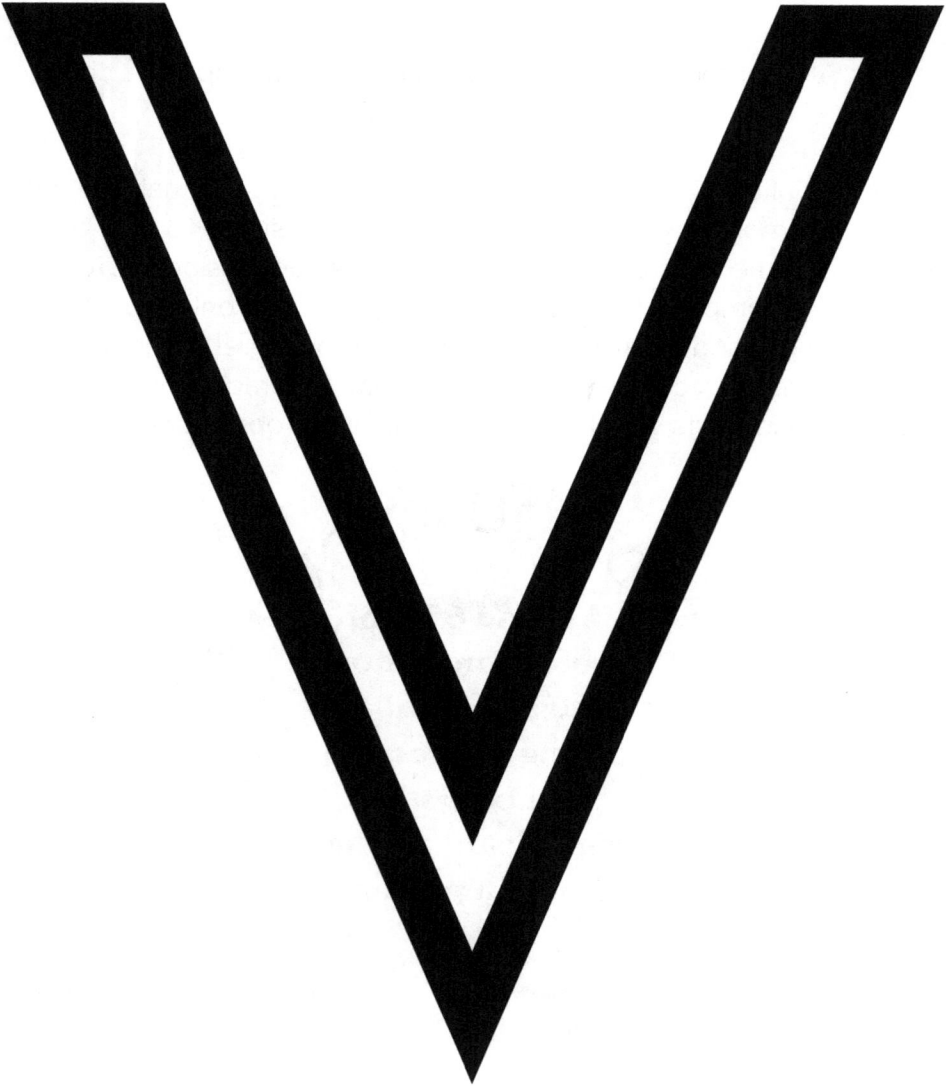

V

70. VIDEO CONTENT

Video content has become increasingly important on LinkedIn™ for engaging audiences, showcasing expertise, and enhancing brand presence. Just as a disco party comes alive with dynamic visuals and music, video content can bring your LinkedIn™ profile and company page to life. LinkedIn was ranked in position 7 in Statista's 2023 study, which looked at the most effective video marketing channels according to marketers worldwide - 59% of respondents found LinkedIn™ to be an effective video-marketing channel.

Why Video Content is Important on LinkedIn®

Higher Engagement
Videos typically generate more likes, comments, and shares than text-based posts. Some reports suggest that video content can generate up to 1200% more shares than text and images combined. This is like having a crowd-pleasing dance number that gets everyone on the floor.

Increased Visibility
LinkedIn™'s algorithm favours video content, potentially increasing your reach; it's just like having a spotlight on your performance at the disco.

Showcasing Expertise
Videos allow you to demonstrate your knowledge and skills in a more dynamic way. This is similar to a DJ showcasing their mixing skills live.

Building Trust
Seeing and hearing you or your team members can help build a stronger connection with your audience; it's like the personal connection formed when meeting someone face-to-face at a party.

Types of Video Content for LinkedIn®

1. How-To Videos: Share your expertise by creating tutorials or explainer videos. This is like teaching party-goers a new dance move.

2. Behind-the-Scenes: Give your audience a glimpse into your company culture or processes, just like showing guests the DJ decks at your disco.

V

VIDEO CONTENT

3. Product Demonstrations: Showcase your products or services in action. This is similar to demonstrating the latest party gadgets to your guests.

4. Thought Leadership: Share your insights on industry trends or challenges, in the same way that a DJ might discuss the latest music trends between sets.

5. Client Testimonials: Feature satisfied clients talking about their experience with your company, much like party-goers raving about the great time they're having.

Best Practices for LinkedIn® Video Content

Keep It Short: Aim for videos under 2 minutes to maintain viewer attention. This is like keeping dance tracks short and sweet to maintain energy on the floor.

Use Captions: Many users watch videos without sound, so include captions. This ensures your message gets across, like having visual cues for dancers when the music's too loud.

Start Strong: Grab attention in the first few seconds. This is similar to a DJ starting with a popular track to get people dancing immediately.

Be Authentic: Don't over-produce your videos. Authenticity resonates well on LinkedIn™; it's like a DJ who genuinely enjoys the music they're playing.

Call to Action: End your video with a clear next step for viewers, just like a DJ announcing the next event or special at the end of the night.

Optimise for Mobile: Ensure your videos look good on mobile devices, where most LinkedIn™ users access the platform. This is like ensuring your disco looks great from every angle.

Measuring Video Performance

Use LinkedIn™'s analytics to track views, engagement, and audience retention. This data can help you refine your video strategy, much like a DJ adjusting their playlist based on the crowd's response.

V

VIDEO CONTENT

Incorporating video content into your LinkedIn™ strategy can significantly boost your engagement, visibility, and credibility. By creating diverse, authentic, and valuable video content, you can showcase your expertise and build stronger connections with your audience. Just as a great DJ uses music and visuals to create an unforgettable party experience, your video content can make your LinkedIn™ presence more dynamic and engaging. Embrace the power of video and watch your professional influence grow.

DID YOU KNOW?

LinkedIn® reports that users spent three times more time watching videos than viewing static content.

CHOICE POINTS

If you want to learn more about content strategy, turn to page 34.
To explore more about visibility, turn to page 197.
To delve deeper into posts, go to page 127.

V

72. VISIBILITY

You're hosting the most spectacular disco party, complete with flashing lights, vibrant decorations, and the best music in town. You want everyone to know about it, so they will come and join in the fun. Gaining visibility on LinkedIn™ is just like that; it's about making sure people see you and what you can offer. Here's how it works:

Attracting Attention

Gaining visibility means getting noticed by potential clients and connections; it's like having a massive neon sign outside your party that says: 'Join the Fun'. On LinkedIn™, when people see your posts, articles, and updates, they're more likely to engage with you and learn about your business.

Building Your Reputation

When more people see you, it helps build your reputation as an expert in your field. Just as a packed dance floor shows that your party is the place to be, having a strong presence on LinkedIn™ signals that you're a credible professional. This can lead to more opportunities and connections.

Creating Opportunities

Increased visibility opens doors to new opportunities; it's like when your party gets so much buzz that people start talking about it, and more guests want to join in. On LinkedIn™, being visible can lead to collaborations, partnerships, or new clients who are interested in what you do.

Engaging with Your Audience

Visibility allows you to engage with your audience more effectively. Just as party guests mingle and chat, you can interact with your followers and connections on LinkedIn™. This engagement helps you understand their needs and interests, allowing you to tailor your content and offerings accordingly.

How to Gain Visibility on LinkedIn®

1.Create Quality Content
Share valuable and relevant content regularly. This is like putting up eye-catching decorations at your party that draw people in. Use images, videos, and articles to showcase your expertise and keep your audience engaged.

V

VISIBILITY

2. Participate in Groups

Join LinkedIn™ groups related to your industry. Engaging in discussions is like inviting people to dance at your party; the more you participate, the more people will notice you and your insights.

3. Encourage Employee Advocacy

If you have a team, motivate them to engage with your content. When they like, comment, or share your posts, it's like having your friends spread the word about your fabulous party, attracting even more guests.

4. Use Hashtags Wisely

Incorporate relevant hashtags in your posts. This is like using bright lights to guide people to your party. Hashtags help your content reach a broader audience, making it easier for new connections to find you.

5. Connect with Influencers

Reach out to industry leaders and influencers; building relationships with them can boost your visibility, just like having a famous DJ at your party who draws in the crowd.

Gaining visibility on LinkedIn™ is essential for growing your professional presence and attracting new opportunities. By creating engaging content, participating in groups, and connecting with others, you can ensure that your profile shines as brightly as the disco ball at your party. Now, get out there, make some noise, and let everyone know about the amazing things you have to offer.

Measuring Your Visibility

Use LinkedIn™ analytics to track the performance of your posts and profile views. This data can help you understand what resonates with your audience and adjust your strategy accordingly, much like a DJ monitoring the crowd's reaction to the music.

Increasing your visibility on LinkedIn™ is essential for attracting opportunities, building your network, and establishing your authority in your industry. By optimising your profile, engaging consistently, utilising hashtags, and leveraging LinkedIn™ features, you can enhance your professional presence and stand out in a competitive landscape. Just as a vibrant disco party captures attention and creates lasting memories, a strong LinkedIn™ presence can lead to meaningful connections and professional growth. Embrace these strategies, and watch your visibility and influence expand.

V

VISIBILITY

CHOICE POINTS

If you want to learn more about data insights, turn to page 40.
To explore more about the featured section, turn to page 53.
To delve deeper into your analytics, go to page 10.

TOP TIP
Use the Featured section to showcase your best work, services, or achievements. Positioning your top content here is like having a main stage at your party where the best acts perform.

72. WHO'S VIEWED YOUR PROFILE FEATURE

Imagine LinkedIn™ as a vibrant disco party where everyone is dancing, networking, and making connections. The 'Who's Viewed Your Profile' feature is like the spotlight that shines on you, revealing who's been checking you out on the dance floor. Here's how to use this feature to your advantage;

1. Spotting Potential Dance Partners

When you see who has viewed your profile, it's like noticing who's been eyeing you from across the dance floor. These individuals might be potential leads or partners. Don't hesitate to approach them with a friendly message, just like you would invite someone to join you for a dance. Start a conversation to explore how you can work together.

2. Engaging with Interested Guests

If someone has taken the time to view your profile, it's a sign of interest, like someone nodding their head to the beat of your favourite song. Engage with these viewers by visiting their profiles, giving them a thumbs-up on their skills, or commenting on their posts. This reciprocal engagement can help build rapport and make you more visible in the party atmosphere.

3. Following Up with New Connections

Think of your new connections as fresh faces at the party. If a new connection has viewed your profile, it's a perfect opportunity to send them a message, thanking them for joining the dance. Suggest a chat to discuss mutual interests or potential collaborations, just like inviting them to join you for a drink at the bar.

4. Optimising Your Dance Moves

If you notice a surge in profile views, it might be because of some new dance moves you've introduced, like updating your profile with relevant keywords or a snazzy new photo. Pay attention to what changes have attracted more viewers and keep refining your profile to keep the spotlight on you.

5. Researching Your Fellow Partygoers

Take a moment to check out the profiles of those who have viewed yours. Understanding their backgrounds and interests is like learning about the other dancers at the party. This knowledge can help you tailor your approach and make more meaningful connections.

W

WHO'S VIEWED YOUR PROFILE FEATURE

6. Going Premium for VIP Access

Consider upgrading to LinkedIn™ Premium for a VIP pass to the party. Premium users can see a complete list of viewers from the past 90 days, giving you deeper insights into who's been checking you out. This information can be invaluable for your networking efforts.

7. Tracking Engagement Trends

Regularly monitor who's viewing your profile to identify trends, like noticing which songs get everyone on the dance floor; are certain types of professionals or industries showing interest? Use this information to tailor your content and engagement-strategies to appeal to these groups.

8. Personalising Your Invitations

When reaching out to someone who has viewed your profile, personalise your message based on their profile information. Mention common connections or shared interests, just as you would chat about a favourite song to break the ice. This makes your outreach more relevant and engaging

By effectively using LinkedIn™'s 'Who's Viewed Your Profile' feature, you can navigate the disco party of networking with confidence, building stronger connections and uncovering new opportunities for growth and collaboration. So, put on your dancing shoes and get ready to shine on the LinkedIn™ dance floor.

CHOICE POINTS

If you want to learn more about connections, turn to page 34.
To explore more about connection notes, turn to page 30.
To delve deeper into privacy settings, go to page 134.

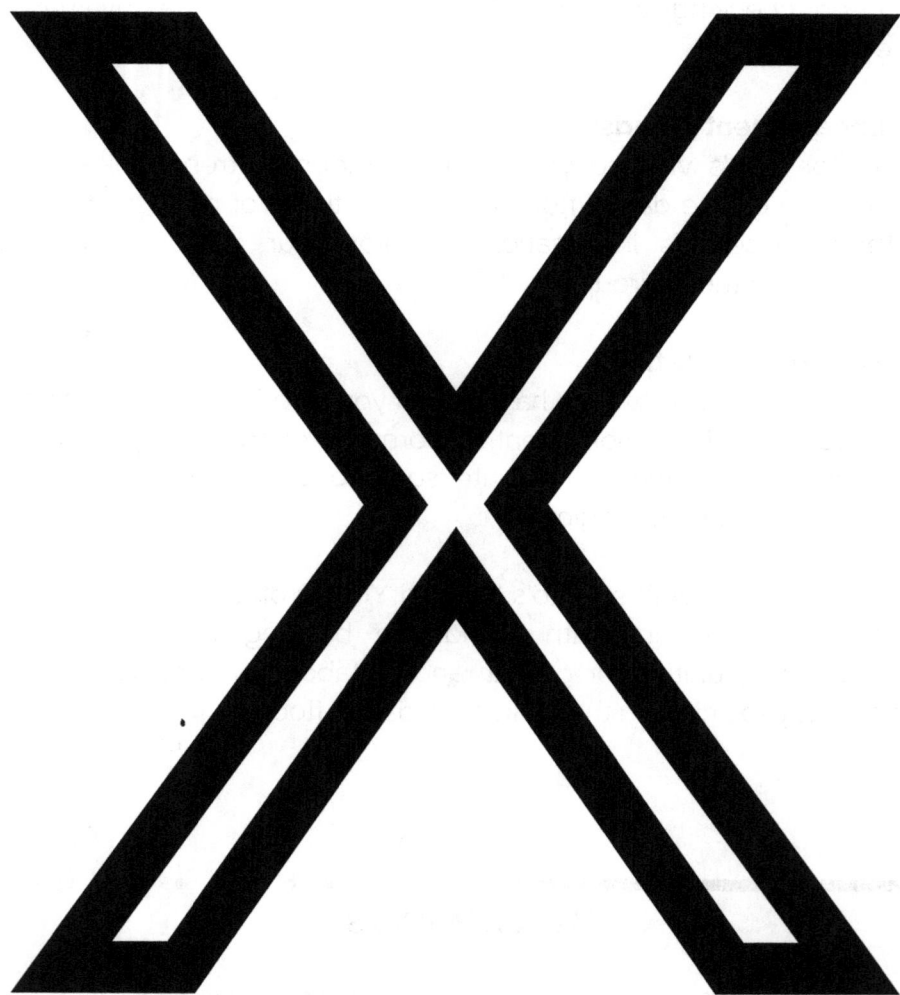

X

74. EXPERIMENTATION

Experimentation on LinkedIn™ is a powerful approach to discovering what works best for your professional growth and engagement. Just as a DJ experiments with different tracks to see what gets the crowd moving, trying out various strategies on LinkedIn™ can help you identify the most effective ways to enhance your presence and achieve your goals. Here's how to approach experimentation on LinkedIn™:

Adaptability

The digital landscape is constantly evolving. Experimentation allows you to stay adaptable and responsive to new trends and changes, much like a DJ adjusting the music to keep the dance floor lively.

Optimisation

By testing different approaches, you can optimise your LinkedIn™ strategy for better results. This is similar to fine-tuning your playlist to ensure maximum enjoyment for your guests.

Innovation

Experimentation encourages creativity and innovation, helping you stand out in a crowded marketplace; it's like introducing new and exciting elements to your party to keep it fresh and engaging.

Strategies for Experimentation on LinkedIn®

1. Content Variation

<u>Try Different Formats:</u> Experiment with various content formats such as articles, videos, infographics, and polls. See which types of content resonate most with your audience. This is like mixing different music genres to see what gets the best response.

<u>Test Posting Times:</u> Post content at different times of the day and week to identify when your audience is most active. This is like playing different tracks at various times to gauge the crowd's reaction.

2. Engagement Techniques

<u>Interactive Posts:</u> Create posts that encourage interaction, such as asking questions or hosting polls. Monitor which approaches generate the most engagement. This is similar to engaging the crowd with shout-outs and interactive elements during a party.

<u>Commenting and Sharing:</u> Experiment with commenting on and sharing content from others in your network. Track how these activities impact your visibility and connections

X

EXPERIMENTATION

3.Profile Optimisation

Headline and Summary: Test different headlines and summaries to see which ones attract more profile views and connections. This is like tweaking your party invitations to make them more appealing.

Skills and Endorsements: Experiment with highlighting different skills and seeking endorsements for them. Monitor which skills attract the most attention and endorsements.

4. Networking Approaches

Personalised Connection Requests: Try different styles of personalised messages when sending connection requests. See which approaches result in higher acceptance rates. This is like trying different conversation starters at a party.

Engaging with Groups: Join various LinkedIn™ groups related to your industry and participate in discussions. Track which groups provide the most valuable connections and insights.

Best Practices for Experimentation

Set Clear Objectives: Define what you aim to achieve with each experiment, whether it's increased engagement, more connections, or enhanced visibility. This is like setting goals for your party, such as attendance numbers or guest satisfaction.

Track and Analyse Results: Use LinkedIn™ analytics to monitor the performance of your experiments. Analyse the data to identify patterns and insights. This is similar to observing the crowd's reaction to different tracks and adjusting your playlist accordingly.

Be Patient and Persistent: Not all experiments will yield immediate results. Be patient and persistent and be prepared to iterate based on your findings. Just like trying out new tracks and refining your setlist over time.

Stay Authentic: While experimenting, ensure that your content and interactions remain authentic and true to your personal brand. Authenticity resonates with your audience, much like a DJ's genuine passion for music enhances their performance.

X

EXPERIMENTATION

Experimentation on LinkedIn™ is essential for discovering the most effective strategies to enhance your professional presence and achieve your goals. By trying different content formats, engagement techniques, profile optimisations, networking approaches, and utilising LinkedIn™ features, you can identify what works best for you. Just as a DJ experiments with different tracks to create the perfect party atmosphere, your willingness to experiment or LinkedIn™ can lead to greater visibility, stronger connections, and professional growth. Embrace the spirit of experimentation and watch your LinkedIn™ presence thrive.

CHOICE POINTS

If you want to learn more about new features, turn to page 103.
To explore more about visibility, turn to page 197.
To find out about analytics, go to page 12.

TOP TIP

Try posting similar content in different formats (e.g., a text post versus a video) and compare their performance. This is like testing two different party themes to see which one draws a bigger crowd.

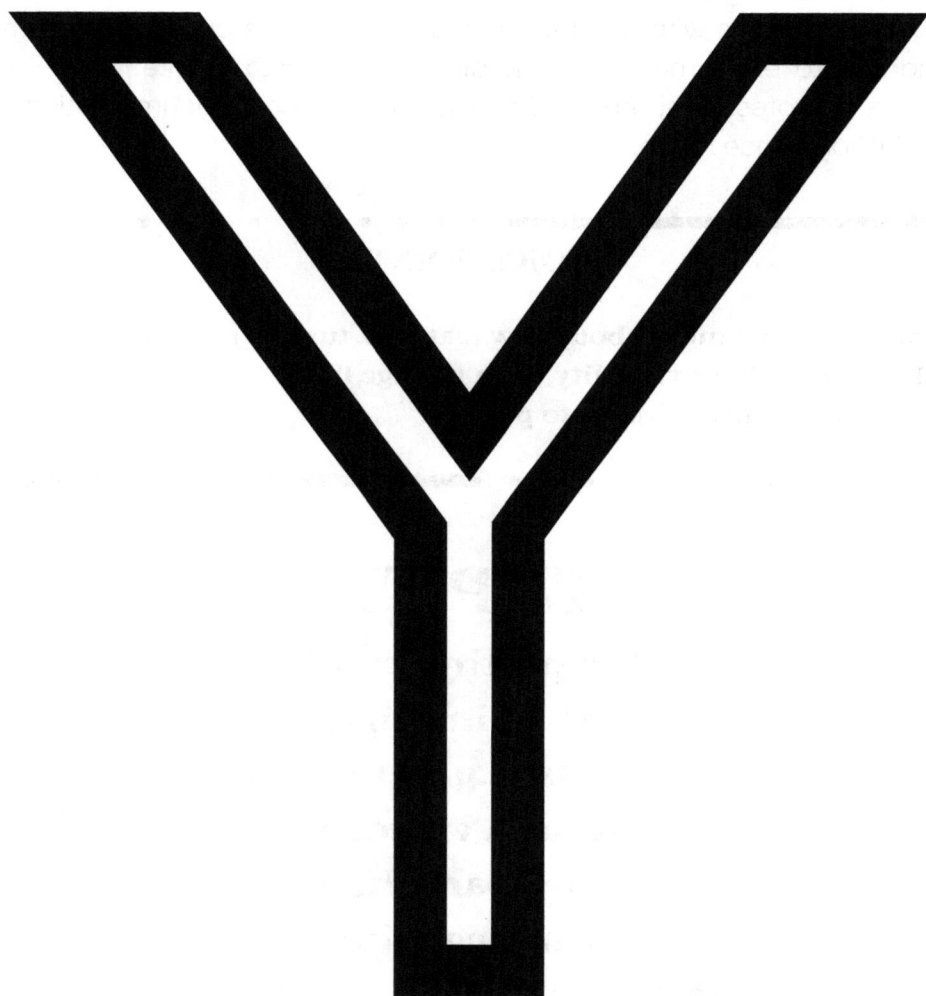

Y

74. YEARLY GOALS

Setting yearly goals on LinkedIn™ is crucial for guiding your professional development and maximising your presence on the platform. Just as a DJ plans their setlist for the year to ensure a memorable experience for their audience, establishing clear goals can help you focus your efforts and measure your progress.

Why Setting Yearly Goals is Important

Direction and Focus

Yearly goals provide a clear direction for your LinkedIn™ activities, helping you stay focused on what matters most. This is similar to a DJ having a theme for their party that keeps the music and atmosphere cohesive.

Measurable Progress

Setting specific, measurable goals allows you to track your progress throughout the year. This is like monitoring the crowd's response to your set and adjusting accordingly.

Motivation and Accountability

Having clear goals can motivate you to engage consistently and hold you accountable for your professional development; it's similar to a DJ preparing for a big event, knowing they need to deliver an exceptional performance.

Enhanced Networking Opportunities

By defining your goals, you can strategically connect with individuals and groups that align with your objectives. This is like inviting specific guests to your party who will enhance the overall experience.

How to Set Effective Yearly Goals on LinkedIn®:
1. Reflect on Your Professional Aspirations
Consider where you want to be in your business by the end of the year. This might include advancing your thought leadership or building a personal brand. This reflection is like a DJ considering the kind of music they want to be known for.

2. Make Your Goals SMART
Ensure your goals are Specific, Measurable, Achievable, Relevant, and Time-bound (SMART). For example, instead of saying, 'I want to connect with more people,' a SMART goal would be: 'I will connect with 50 new professionals in my industry by the end of the year. This clarity is essential for tracking your progress.

Y

YEARLY GOALS

3. Break Down Goals into Actionable Steps
Divide your yearly goals into smaller, manageable tasks. For instance, if your goal is to publish monthly articles, outline a content calendar with topics and deadlines. This is like a DJ planning their setlist in advance, ensuring a smooth flow throughout the event.

4. Engage with Your Network
Set goals for engaging with your connections. This could include commenting on a certain number of posts weekly or reaching out to specific individuals for collaboration. This engagement is like a DJ interacting with the crowd to keep the energy high.

5. Monitor and Adjust
Regularly review your progress towards your goals and adjust your strategies as needed. If something isn't working, be flexible enough to change your approach. This is similar to a DJ reading the room and adapting their set based on the crowd's response.

6. Celebrate Milestones
Acknowledge and celebrate your achievements along the way, whether big or small. This recognition can keep you motivated and engaged in your goals; it's like a DJ celebrating a successful set with the audience, creating a memorable experience.

Examples of Yearly Goals for LinkedIn®

Networking Goals: Connect with 100 new professionals in your industry and engage with at least 10 of them each month.

Content Creation Goals: Publish one article per month and share relevant posts weekly to showcase your expertise.

Skill Development Goals: Complete three online courses related to your field and share insights from each course with your network.

Engagement Goals: Actively participate in five LinkedIn™ groups and contribute to discussions at least once a week.

Thought Leadership Goals: Host a LinkedIn™ Live session or webinar on a relevant topic by the end of the year.

Y

YEARLY GOALS

Setting yearly goals on LinkedIn™ is essential for guiding your professional development and maximising your presence on the platform. By reflecting on your aspirations, making your goals SMART, breaking them down into actionable steps, engaging with your network, monitoring your progress, and celebrating milestones, you can create a clear roadmap for success. Just as a DJ plans their set to create an unforgettable experience, your strategic approach to LinkedIn™ can lead to meaningful connections and professional growth. Embrace the process of goal-setting, and watch your LinkedIn™ presence flourish throughout the year.

CHOICE POINTS

If you want to learn more about strategy, turn to page 169.
To explore more about analytics, turn to page 10.
To delve deeper into thought leadership, go to page 182.

TOP TIP
When you reach your goals, take the time to celebrate your successes. This is like throwing a mini after-party to acknowledge the great time everyone had, reinforcing your motivation for future goals.

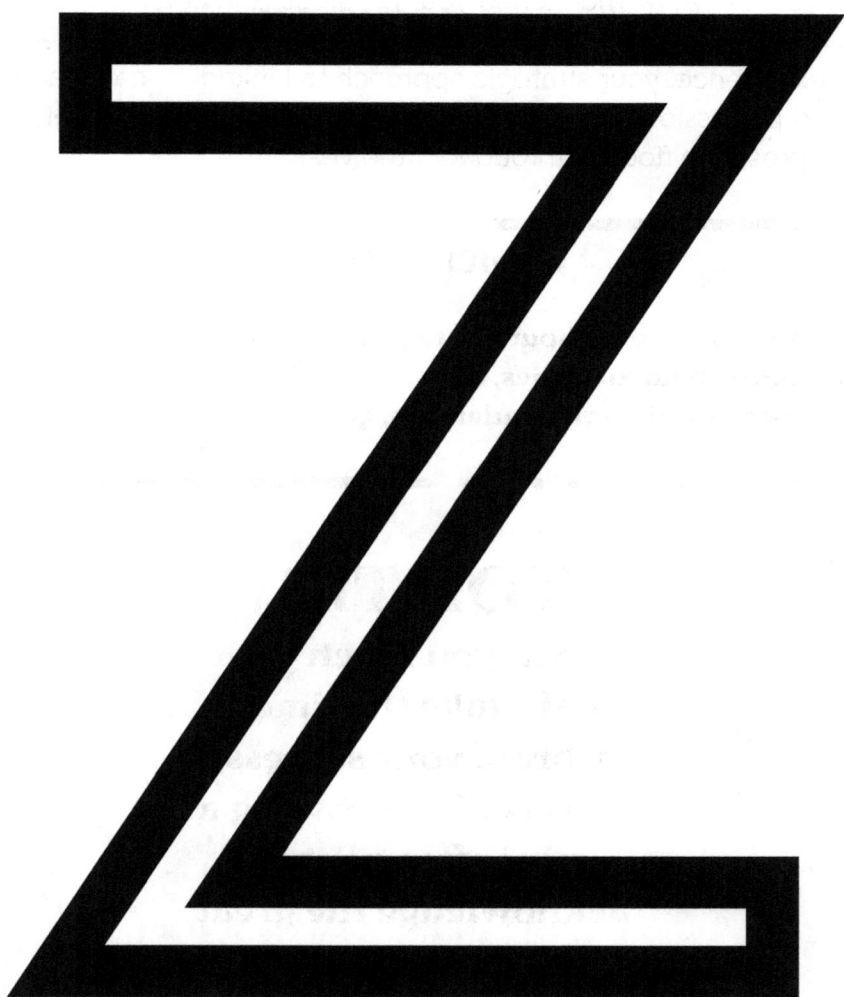

Z

75. ZERO TO HERO

The journey from 'zero to hero' on LinkedIn™ involves strategically building your profile, expanding your network, and establishing yourself as a thought leader in your industry. Just as a DJ evolves from playing small gigs to headlining major events, you can elevate your presence on LinkedIn™ through consistent effort and smart strategies. Here's how to make that transformation.

1. Optimise Your Profile

Your LinkedIn™ profile is your digital business card and the first impression potential connections will have of you.

Professional Photo: Use a high-quality, professional photo that reflects your personal brand. This is like having a memorable photo for your DJ persona that draws people in.

Compelling Headline: Craft a headline that clearly states what you do and what sets you apart. Instead of just listing your job title, consider including your unique value proposition.

Detailed Summary: Write a summary that tells your story, highlights your achievements, and showcases your skills. This is similar to sharing your journey as a DJ, detailing how you got started and what makes your sets unique.

2. Create Engaging Content

Regularly sharing valuable content can position you as a thought leader and attract more connections.

Thought Leadership Articles: Write articles that showcase your expertise and insights on industry trends. This is like a DJ releasing a mix tape that showcases their unique sound and style.

Video Content: Incorporate video into your strategy. Videos are proven to capture attention and can significantly boost engagement. Share insights, tutorials, or behind-the-scenes looks at your work. As noted, video content is highly effective on LinkedIn™, making it a powerful tool for connection and engagement.

Use Eye-Catching Visuals: Enhance your posts with images or infographics to make them more appealing. Just as a DJ uses vibrant visuals to enhance the party experience, strong visuals can make your content stand out in the feed.

Z

ZERO TO HERO

3. Engage with Your Network

Building relationships is key to expanding your reach on LinkedIn™.

Comment and Share: Actively engage with posts from your connections and industry leaders. Thoughtful comments can spark conversations and increase your visibility.

Join Relevant Groups: Participate in LinkedIn™ groups related to your industry. This allows you to connect with like-minded professionals and share your insights, similar to networking with other DJs at industry events.

Personalised Connection Requests: When sending connection requests, personalise your message to make it more meaningful. This is like introducing yourself to someone new at a party and making a genuine connection.

4. Leverage LinkedIn® Features

Utilising LinkedIn's features can enhance your visibility and engagement.

For example, use polls to engage your audience and gather insights. This is similar to asking party-goers what songs they want to hear next, making them feel involved in the experience.

5. Measure and Adjust

Regularly review your LinkedIn analytics to track your progress and adjust your strategy accordingly.

Monitor Engagement: Pay attention to which types of content generate the most engagement. This feedback is invaluable for refining your approach, similar to a DJ adjusting their set based on crowd reactions.

Set SMART Goals: Establish Specific, Measurable, Achievable, Relevant, and Time-bound goals for your LinkedIn™ activities. This will help you stay focused and motivated on your journey from zero to hero.

Z

ZERO TO HERO

Transforming your LinkedIn™ presence from zero to hero requires a strategic approach that involves optimising your profile, creating engaging content, actively engaging with your network, leveraging LinkedIn™'s features, and continually measuring your progress. By following these steps, you can elevate your professional presence and establish yourself as a thought leader in your industry. Just as a DJ evolves through practise and experimentation, your commitment to enhancing your LinkedIn™ profile will lead to greater visibility, stronger connections, and new opportunities. Embrace the journey and watch your LinkedIn™ presence flourish.

CHOICE POINTS

If you want to learn more about goal setting, turn to page 208.
To explore more about your target audience, turn to page 177.
To delve deeper into your content strategy, go to page 34.

TOP TIP

Determine the specific topics that align with your expertise and interests that will add value to your target audience. Just as a disco has a theme, your content should focus on areas where you can provide the most value.

Index

Index

Index

Index

About the Author

Esther Partridge-Warner is a distinguished academic and business professional with a diverse background in education and digital technology. She graduated in 2005 with a joint honours degree in IT and Education, subsequently earning a Postgraduate Certificate in Learning and Teaching for Higher Education.

Her academic career has been marked by notable positions at prestigious institutions. She has contributed her expertise to the Business School at the University of Worcester and the University of Worcester International College. Currently, Esther lectures on the master's programme at the University of Roehampton, where she specialises in Social Media and Influencers.

Beyond her academic pursuits, Esther has established herself as an award-winning business coach. She works closely with business owners and leaders, guiding them towards building successful organisations. Her approach combines theoretical knowledge with practical insights, enabling her clients to achieve tangible results.

In her book, 'A to Z: Everything You Need to Know about LinkedIn® for Business Owners & Leaders', Esther seamlessly blends her academic expertise with her practical business acumen. This comprehensive guide reflects her passion for helping professionals harness the power of LinkedIn® for business growth.

Esther's enthusiasm for her work is evident in her own words: "I love nothing more than seeing my clients consistently win business from LinkedIn®, mastering the platform for consistent growth."

Her dedication to empowering business leaders through digital platforms continues to inspire and drive success in the ever-evolving landscape of professional networking.

To work with Esther visit onlinemediaworks.co.uk